How to Settle a
Simple Estate
Without a Lawyer

The Complete Guide to Wills, Probate, and Inheritance Law Explained Simply

(With Companion CD-ROM)

Linda C. Ashar, *Attorney at Law*

HOW TO SETTLE A SIMPLE ESTATE WITHOUT A LAWYER: THE COMPLETE GUIDE TO WILLS, PROBATE, AND INHERITANCE LAW EXPLAINED SIMPLY (WITH COMPANION CD-ROM)

Copyright © 2013 Atlantic Publishing Group, Inc.
1210 SW 23rd Place • Ocala, Florida 34471 • Phone 800-814-1132 • Fax 352-622-1875
Website: www.atlantic-pub.com • Email: sales@atlantic-pub.com
SAN Number: 268-1250

Library of Congress Cataloging-in-Publication Data

Ashar, Linda C., 1947-
  How to settle a simple estate without a lawyer: the complete guide to wills, probate, and inheritance law explained simply : with companion CD-ROM / by Linda C. Ashar.
     p. cm.
  Includes bibliographical references and index.
  ISBN 978-1-60138-614-4 (alk. paper) -- ISBN 1-60138-614-1 (alk. paper) 1. Estate planning--United States. 2. Probate law and practice--United States. 3. Wills--United States. 4. Inheritance and succession--United States. I. Title.
  KF750.Z9A79 2012
  332.024'0160973--dc23
                                    2012025177

Printed in the United States

Printed on Recycled Paper

INTERIOR LAYOUT: Antoinette D'Amore • addesign@videotron.ca
PROOFREADING: C&P Marse • bluemoon6749@bellsouth.net
COVER DESIGNS: Jackie Miller • millerjackiej@gmail.com

A few years back we lost our beloved pet dog Bear, who was not only our best and dearest friend but also the "Vice President of Sunshine" here at Atlantic Publishing. He did not receive a salary but worked tirelessly 24 hours a day to please his parents.

Bear was a rescue dog who turned around and showered myself, my wife, Sherri, his grandparents Jean, Bob, and Nancy, and every person and animal he met (well, maybe not rabbits) with friendship and love. He made a lot of people smile every day.

We wanted you to know a portion of the profits of this book will be donated in Bear's memory to local animal shelters, parks, conservation organizations, and other individuals and nonprofit organizations in need of assistance.

– *Douglas & Sherri Brown*

PS: We have since adopted two more rescue dogs: first Scout, and the following year, Ginger. They were both mixed golden retrievers who needed a home.

Want to help animals and the world? Here are a dozen easy suggestions you and your family can implement today:

- *Adopt and rescue a pet from a local shelter.*
- *Support local and no-kill animal shelters.*
- *Plant a tree to honor someone you love.*
- *Be a developer — put up some birdhouses.*
- *Buy live, potted Christmas trees and replant them.*
- *Make sure you spend time with your animals each day.*
- *Save natural resources by recycling and buying recycled products.*
- *Drink tap water, or filter your own water at home.*
- *Whenever possible, limit your use of or do not use pesticides.*
- *If you eat seafood, make sustainable choices.*
- *Support your local farmers market.*
- *Get outside. Visit a park, volunteer, walk your dog, or ride your bike.*

Five years ago, Atlantic Publishing signed the Green Press Initiative. These guidelines promote environmentally friendly practices, such as using recycled stock and vegetable-based inks, avoiding waste, choosing energy-efficient resources, and promoting a no-pulping policy. We now use 100-percent recycled stock on all our books. The results: in one year, switching to post-consumer recycled stock saved 24 mature trees, 5,000 gallons of water, the equivalent of the total energy used for one home in a year, and the equivalent of the greenhouse gases from one car driven for a year.

Acknowledgments

Huge appreciation and grateful thanks goes to the Lorain County Probate Court of Ohio, Honorable James Walther, for having its Court forms and other estate information available on the Internet for the public and practitioners. I also appreciate and thank all the many other jurists and courts around the country, many used as reference for this book, who possess the creative foresight and dedication to make the legal process user-friendly for the public they serve. Professional legal advice is important and an attorney's representation has a place in assisting non-lawyers in court, but the process of law in our judicial system should be available to all people.

Dedication

"For my family"

Table of Contents

Chapter 9:
Taxes..**209**

Chapter 10:
Settling and Closing the Estate..............................**219**

Conclusion **233**

Introduction

*I*t was Benjamin Franklin who coined the well-known adage, "nothing is certain but death and taxes." The fiduciary of a decedent's estate deals with both these certainties and many other things as well.

In modern society, every person who dies leaves something to be handled by the living. In many cases, a person leaves property, personal possessions, final wishes to be resolved, and loose ends to be tied up. Some people prepare in advance and organize the process for those left behind; others do not. Regardless of the decedent's forethought, it falls to someone to take charge and manage these final affairs. Depending on the specific facts and local court procedure involved, this person is known as the decedent's estate's personal representative, executor (man) or executrix (woman), administrator, or other similar title conferred by the probate court. The general term, applicable in all cases, is "personal representative" or "estate representative," the terms used in this book.

The decedent's property owned at time of death is called an estate. The estate's personal representative is appointed to represent the estate officially and finalize the decedent's affairs. The news media often report about high profile, complex estates, such as that of the late George Steinbrenner, owner of the New York Yankees, but most people leave estates far simpler by comparison. This book is intended as a guide for the personal representative of the simple estate. It will provide the reader an overview of the typical, basic considerations that arise in planning and administering estates.

CASE STUDY: EDITH'S STORY, SURPRISING SECRET

by Attorney X
(Fictional names used to
protect privacy and confidentiality)

Dealing with remains of a person's life can sound cut and dried, perhaps even tedious. After all, it is a process of lists. Collect the necessary paper, take an inventory of the deceased's belongings, list who is owed money, list who has rights by law and by will to the property in the estate, and then it is just a matter of dispensing with the lists in the right order. Line up the beneficiaries and tell them where they stand; pay the bills; dole out the property; dust off one's hands — done. Right?

Well, in a sense that is a quick summary of the essentials. All of it has to be done by law, through the court process, but in essence, it is a process of organization and accountability of property, payment of debts, and distribution of the remaining property to the lawful heirs. However, a *life* is rarely that simple. When a person dies, he or she leaves behind a personal story and often, secrets. The story revealed to the estate representative can be shocking, difficult, and emotional, especially when dealing with the effects upon family.

Edith, an independent widow, came to me for assistance in handling her brother Edward's estate. Edward, a retired accountant, had never married, had no children, and owned his own home. Edith thought she probably could handle most of what needed to be done but wanted some guidance on the procedure of the estate. She could not find a will. Although this seemed out of character for Edward, who as an accountant understood the importance of estate planning, it is not unusual. Seventy percent of Americans do not have valid wills.

Edith was the sole heir at law to inherit Edward's estate, as only her own children were other surviving relatives in the family. The law of every state provides how property will be distributed when there is no will. The law is called the statute of descent and distribution. Spouse and children of the deceased and then their children are first considered. Then come the deceased's parents and siblings and in turn their children. In this case, Edward's next of kin was Edith, his sibling. So other than valuing the assets of his estate and determining debts and taxes, managing Edward's estate seemed it would be a straightforward process for Edith.

Edith was upset by the loss of her brother, but they had not been particularly close in their adult lives. Edward was several years older than Edith; she described him as a workaholic. He apparently had done well with his own accounting practice and had seemed to be enjoying his retirement because he traveled often. They would have dinner together about once a month, and he would join her family on most holidays, though he usually took a trip over the December holidays, "to recharge his batteries for tax season," he would tell her before he retired. It was shortly after his return from a trip that Edward died of a heart attack.

We opened an estate for Edward. He had bank accounts, real estate, and various artifacts of possible value in his house that would need to be transferred through the court. His car was leased. As Edith was his sole legal heir, having her appointed administrator was no problem. Once Edith was set up as administratrix of the estate, she felt comfortable proceeding with the process on her own. She said she would call me if she had a question.

It was when Edith started to inventory Edward's house that the call came. The brother she thought she knew was not the man who lived in the comfortable brick mock Tudor tucked into a cul-de-sac of the city suburb. Edith called to ask me to meet her at the house soon. Her voice was not the usual robust no-nonsense Edith. She would not explain her distress on the phone. I could meet her the next day, I told her.

In Edward's house, Edith had found a hidden room of sorts — and another Edward — in plain sight, in his office. Edith showed me beautiful enclosed oak cabinets that lined the walls with locked doors. Edith had found the keys on Edward's personal key ring. These oak cupboards contained hundreds of leather-covered journals filled with Edward's precise writing, books, photographs, and videotapes. The journals contained explicit detailed accounts of Edward's sexual experiences during his many travels and apparently as part of his association with a private club that engaged in a variety of sado-masochistic sexual parties in various parts of the world. The videos represented a timeline of Edward's activities; numerous private videotapes and DVDs documented personal activities and professionally made productions. The books ranged from those of art quality photographic publications to genre S&M fiction and graphic, sexually explicit photographs. Some of these involved people of both sexes, others, homosexual males. The presence of the journals and the photos in which Edward himself appeared, either with other men, or with younger people of both sexes, that completely undid Edith. Drawers behind Edward's locked doors contained amazing wide variety of sexual paraphernalia.

Edith wanted to have a bonfire on the spot. She was angry, but I could not tell which aspect of the situation upset her the most: her brother's secrecy, his activities, the photographs, the videos, or the journals. One thing was clear. Behind the oak doors was an Edward Edith never knew. His lifestyle was as undeniable as it was a secret to his sister.

Edith was shaken with shock and emotion. She and her brother had not been close in their day-to-day lives, but he was her older brother, and she loved him. She felt betrayed and naïve by the discovery of Edward's "other life." She could not understand his reasons for hiding his lifestyle from her. Because she would not approve and have worried? Because he was ashamed of it? Because he did not care for her feelings or because he did? I listened to her go through these questions, sympathizing with her agony and her anger, and knowing that unless we found something written by Edward himself, there was unlikely to ever be answers to her questions. I suggested she might find some insight among his journals; perhaps among the records of the prurient activities he had also recorded other kinds of secret personal thoughts that might reveal something meaningful to his sister. I doubted, though, if she could get past the secrecy and subject matter. Edith did not want to touch any of it. She had shut and locked the oak doors. Then she asked me what to do.

I told her first we needed to be sure there was no evidence of crime. Though I doubted it, anything was possible. One huge surprise might lead to another. The first cursory look at Edward's "secret room" had not revealed anything illegal. There was no evidence he was engaged in activities involving sex slavery, nonconsensual physical harm, forced sexual activity, or any activity involving minors. Because he apparently had spent a good part of his adult life in this lifestyle, primarily in his travels out of the country, according to the timeline shown by the materials he kept, very little of his lifestyle occurred at his home. If so, he had been very discreet. It was not likely that Edward would have been involved in illegal activity for such a long time while escaping exposure. Still, as officers of the court — Edith as appointed personal representative and I as an attorney — we were required to exercise due diligence. The reason for due diligence as to crime was of course no longer a concern for Edward, the deceased, but rather as to whether his records disclosed evidence of any crime committed by others still living, or whether there was any relevance to crimes unsolved.

Second, I explained to Edith that although her brother's collection was abhorrent to her, it had to be valued as part of the estate. Fortunately, review of Edward's secret collection revealed no evidence of crime. It disclosed the careful documentation of a grown man's obsession with a certain lifestyle that he had compartmentalized within his life, and his compulsion to keep his lifestyle a secret from his family and colleagues, literally in the closet. His collection disclosed nothing of illegal sales or illegal making of pornographic videos or photos. Discreet inquiries indicated that the contents of Edward's closet did not have any special intrinsic "collectable" value either. Although Edith was not about to sell any of it, had there been a collectable value to any of Edward's hidden artifacts, the value would have been listed on the estate inventory, probably as an "S&M genre collection" with the appraiser's value. Ultimately, Edward's "collection" was not itemized in the inventory of the estate. It was included as part of with "miscellaneous personal effects." Edith had inherited her brother's collection and what she did with it was her decision and her business. When the estate was closed, I never asked her, though I suspected she may have had her bonfire.

Edith's story is not that unusual insofar as surprises can be revealed about a person after death. There is often more to handle in an estate than property and forms. There are people and with people come the full range of human deeds and emotions that go with them. Edith suffered first the shock and grief of her brother's sudden death, and then the exponential aggravation of those emotions with anger, surprise, bewilderment, questioning, and concerns that arose from the discovery that Edward led a life he scrupulously kept a secret from her. Starting out to handle his estate on her own, she confronted something she could not handle legally or emotionally. In this situation, she did obtain legal counsel for those aspects of the estate that were beyond her capabilities to manage. A significant part of assisting Edith with estate management was helping her deal with Edward's secret life.

Although the focus of this book is the simple estate, nothing is "simple," that is not understood. Handling the business matters of an estate invokes a multitude of details that are potentially frustrating and emotionally exhausting, especially, as is usually the case for the personal representative, if the decedent was someone close — a spouse, relative, or dear friend. Further, as in Edith's case, the deceased might have left a surprise lurking in the shadows for the personal representative to handle. The management of these situations involves much more than allocating property to the correct column and adding and subtracting correctly. It is also more than following court procedure and filing the correct forms at the right time — important though these things are. It might also involve balancing emotions and demands of surviving family members.

CASE STUDY: THE MADISON ESTATE, FAMILY GREED

by Attorney X
(Fictional names used to
protect privacy and confidentiality)

When a family member dies, particularly a parent, or perhaps a maiden aunt, family members can descend like vultures to seize the items they want from the deceased's belongings, often in contradiction the terms of a will or gifts made by the deceased before dying. An example is the case of the estate of Maxx Madison. Maxx was a widower with three children. There was Marlow Madison, the farmer son who lived two miles down the road and Marlow's wife Chlorice. There was Adele Madison, Maxx's musical teacher daughter, unmarried; and April, Maxx's married daughter, a local store owner with her husband Carlo. None of these adult children was doing too badly financially.

Before Maxx died, during his last year he was not well, and Marlow and Chlorice took care of him, helping with meals, his housecleaning and looking after his dog, Barley, when he needed to go to the vet. Adele would stop by on Sunday afternoons a couple times a month. April and Carlo were feuding with Maxx because he refused to give them his 1957 Chevy to restore. When Maxx died, they had not seen him for a year.

Maxx left a will dividing all his property evenly among the three children, with the exception of the following special bequests of the Chevy to Marlow (worth $10,000 before restoration), the family grand piano to Adele (worth $30,000), and his coin collection (worth $25,000) to Chlorice "in appreciation for her care and help." He named Marlow the executor.

Before the will was published, while everyone was at the gathering following the funeral, at the church hall, Carlo slipped out, went to Maxx's house with his pickup truck, and took the coin collection, a gun collection, all the collectable chinaware, the antique dining table and chairs, three paintings, and ten first-edition books. Carlo hid the coin collection in a bank vault and the other items in his and April's store warehouse.

When Marlow began the inventory for the estate, he knew right away that these items were missing because he was familiar with his father's house and contents. He suspected Carlo took the items, but had no proof. He filed a police report and told the police he suspected Carlo and April because they had been feuding with Maxx before he died, and Carlo was seen leaving the funeral early. Eventually, the property was recovered, but Carlo argued he was entitled to take things so long as they did not exceed his wife's one-third interest. Aside from the fact he and April were unaware they were getting anything under a will, this is not how division would work. First, the coin collection was a specific bequest for Chlorice. It was not part of the division among the three children. Second, the items of the estate have to be appraised to determine the valuation for dividing it into thirds. Some of the one-third distribution to each could be done with "in kind" items (that is, with actual item rather than selling it and getting the cash), but only if all three agree. In Maxx's Estate, Marlow had to have the court hold a hearing to determine how the property division should be handled because the three siblings could not agree. The court ordered that the car be given to Marlow and the coin collection to Chlorice as the will stated. Everything else was sold at auction and the net proceeds divided equally among the three siblings.

Dealing with family and other beneficiaries can be complicated, and often, actions are motivated by grief, greed, or both. It is the personal representative's responsibility to understand competing emotions and motivations and maintain equilibrium. Not every estate is acrimonious, but by definition of the circumstances, the process is not activated by a happy occasion. In the culture of death and probate, a good process is one that proceeds orderly and peacefully.

Any of the following can be some of the concerns faced by the personal representative:

- *Immediate concerns:* Who is handling the funeral arrangements? What are the decedent's wishes for burial/cremation or organ/body donation? Is there a coroner report involved? Is the burial local or out of state? How many certified copies of the death certificate should be obtained?

- *Finding and organizing "paper":* Is there a will? Is the will document the original will? Is there more than one version of the will? Are there codicils (additions made to the will)? How old is the will (which means there could be changes in property, living heirs, and persons named in the will since it was written)? Where is the car title(s), and is it in the decedent's name? Is there a safety deposit box? Are there bank accounts? Are there other financial accounts and/or holdings? Are there uncashed checks payable to the decedent? Where is the decedent's mail being delivered? Are there any pending business matters or uncompleted contracts of the decedent? Did anyone owe the decedent money that is documented in writing (e.g., promissory notes, contracts)? Was the decedent party to a pending lawsuit or other proceeding? Are the decedent's past tax returns and financial records available? Is there an ethical will?

- *The Main Residence:* Is the main family home in the decedent's name if owned or is decedent the primary lessee on the lease if rented?

- *Creditors:* Who was owed money by the decedent at time of death? Is the funeral bill paid? Is there danger of any property of the decedent being repossessed? Are there sufficient assets to pay debts? Is there a mortgage? Are there medical bills relating to the decedent's last illness?

- *Debtors:* Who owed money to the decedent at the time of death, and therefore to the estate, such as arrearage of alimony or child support or personal loans the decedent made?

- *Immediate obligations:* With respect to creditors, are there immediate (and/or ongoing) bills owed by the decedent, such as utilities, rent, mortgage, and insurance coverage on property or vehicles? Did the decedent have automatic payments and/or services set up that need to be stopped? With respect to money owed to decedent, are automatic payments being made to the decedent that are supposed to cease on death?

- *Family:* Is there a surviving spouse? Are there any surviving minor children of decedent? Do the spouse and/or minor children require immediate care or attention? Are there guardianship issues relating to the minor children or other dependents of the decedent?

- *Initial Inventory:* What did the decedent own at time of death, and where is it? Is there probate property (property subject to reporting to the probate court)? Non-probate property (property that transfers by law outside the probate court jurisdiction)? Consider: bank accounts, other accounts, stocks, bonds, jewelry, collectibles, furniture, other personal property, and real property — within and outside of decedent's state of residence.

- *Other people:* Who are the potential claimants of the estate? Who are the heirs by law? Are there heirs in addition to the decedent's spouse or children, or other relatives? Are there missing heirs? Are there children not yet born? Are there illegitimate children? Are there beneficiaries of the estate named in the will who are not family members? Are there charitable contributions directed in the will? Did the decedent have employees (separate from any incorporated business)?

- *Trusts:* Is there an existing trust? Is there a testamentary trust (a trust created by the will)? What type of trust? What was the decedent's role in the trust (creator, trustee, beneficiary)? Who are the beneficiaries of the trust? Who is the trustee(s)? How does the trust relate to the probate estate (if at all)?

- *Insurance:* Is there life insurance, such as a policy, credit card insurance, mortgage insurance, accidental death, that has any relation to the estate? The cause of decedent's death may have a bearing on these. Who are the beneficiaries?

- *Taxes:* What tax returns must be filed? Do you have copies of decedent's previous tax returns? Is the estate of high enough estimated value to require federal estate tax filing?

(Currently $5.12 million.) Does your state require estate taxes, and if so, is the estate of sufficient estimated value to require either estate tax or inheritance tax? *Tables in Appendix A of this book indicate estate tax and inheritance tax requirements by state.*

- *Keys:* Who has keys to the decedent's house(s)? Rental properties? Vehicles? Safety deposit box(es)? Storage facility?

- *Records:* Where are decedent's financial and other records, if any? Property deeds? Vehicle titles? Was there a living will or advance directive? Had decedent given anyone power of attorney that was exercised? Although a living will and power of attorney cease to have effect upon death, decisions made pursuant to these documents before death may have a bearing on estate matters.

- *Probate proceedings:* Must a probate action be filed with the court? What court has jurisdiction? What kind of estate should be filed? Are there online forms and other information provided by the court? Where is the courthouse? What is the phone number of the probate court?

How this Book Can Help You

This book is intended to help you deal with these and many other questions that will likely arise. Though the legal requirements differ among the states in terms of laws and procedures for processing estates, taxes, and rules of inheritance, more commonalities exist than differences. The many similarities are emphasized here. However, as previously mentioned, probating estates in compliance with the applicable laws can be complicated, depending on the facts and circumstances. Even with the help of this book, you might encounter some instances in which a lawyer and/or accountant's assistance will be necessary for legal compliance or helpful for your peace of mind, despite your resolve to manage on your own.

Whether counsel is engaged for all or just some part of the estate management, the purpose of this book is to provide a solid understanding of what goes into being an estate representative, demystify routine procedures, and offer guidance to make an informed decision about if and when an attorney is needed. It also will be helpful for understanding the process, even if an attorney is assisting. Case studies are included throughout the book for illustration and additional information about the subjects covered.

The CD-ROM companion to this book and the Appendix contain illustrative samples of the many forms relating to the probate of an estate, as well as a sample will, charts, checklists, and other useful information to help you stay organized while settling the

estate. These are tools to be considered in a "generic" sense because every court has its own rules, requirements, nuances, and preferences for procedures.

Nothing in this book shall be taken as a substitute for specific legal advice in any given matter or in any specific estate or situation. The information provided in this book is based on the laws and procedures in place at the time this book is written. All laws and tax regulations are subject to change by legislatures and agencies at any time and are always subject to court interpretation. As well, courts periodically change their rules, forms, and procedures. Therefore, with this understanding this book can be offered for general information and assistance.

General terminology

Several terms, such as the following, are common within estate discussions and are frequently used in this book. A general glossary also is included for your reference at the end of this book to help with words you might encounter when managing an estate.

- *Administrator/Administratrix:* A person who dies without a valid will is said to be "intestate." Without a valid will, the decedent will not have been able to name his or her own personal representative to manage his or her estate. In such a situation, if a probate estate is opened with a court, the law requires the court to appoint a personal representative. In many states, this appointed person is called the administrator if a man, administratrix if a woman.

- *Codicil:* An amendment to an existing will that changes something in the will is called a codicil. To be valid, a codicil must be executed in the same way as a will must be done according to the law in the state in which it is written.

- *Executor/executrix:* This term is given to the personal representative named by the decedent in the last will and testament to represent the estate. A man is the executor. A woman is the executrix.

- *Fiduciary:* All estate representatives and trustees of trusts, whatever their bestowed title, are fiduciaries of the estate. A fiduciary carries a special, or heightened, duty of honesty and care for the estate or trust and its beneficiaries, which is referred to as a "fiduciary duty."

- *Intestate:* This is the status of the estate when the decedent dies without a valid will. The decedent is said to have died intestate. State law directs how the intestate estate should be handled and to whom the property is distributed. The court appoints the estate's personal representative.

- *Personal representative:* This general term refers to the person who represents the decedent's estate, with or without a will. This person acts on behalf of the estate. He or she represents the decedent, not the beneficiaries or the heirs, not the creditors or the debtors, of the estate. He or she is paid a fee from the estate for his or her services, which can be waived if desired.

- *Probate:* This is the process by which assets of the decedent are passed to the estate's beneficiaries under administration of the estate's personal representative, subject to court supervision, according to state law and the local court's procedures. The court's role is to ensure the assets are collected, the beneficiaries (or heirs if the decedent was intestate) receive their lawful share of the estate, the creditors of the estate are paid, and, if there is a will, that the decedent's intent is carried out to the extent possible.

- *Testate:* This is the status of the estate when the decedent dies with a valid will that directs how the estate should be handled (subject to and as supplemented by state law). The decedent is said to have died testate.

- *Testator:* Person who is author of his or her own will, the decedent

- *Trust:* A legal arrangement that places a defined body of property (the trust "res") such as cash, stocks, bonds, real estate in safekeeping for the benefit of another (the trust "beneficiary") according to the terms and conditions of the trust. The property can be held passively until the trust provides for it to be given to the beneficiary, or it might be managed by the terms of the trust to generate income that is periodically paid to the beneficiary during the term of the trust. *Trusts are explained in Chapter 7 of this book.*

- *Trustee:* Person who manages assets held in trust for the benefit of another person

Refer to the Glossary at the back of the book for other unfamiliar terms.

Chapter 1

Can You Handle an Estate without a Lawyer?

Representatives of large estates, especially estates with complex situations and legal issues involved, usually will need the help of legal counsel to manage them successfully. Also, the procedures and requirements of a specific court might be too difficult to navigate without legal counsel or might even require legal representation. Texas courts, for example, require a lawyer on record with the court on behalf of the estate, even though the law does not expressly require it. A few states require that legal counsel be retained for the estate.

An estate might begin simply but evolve into complications, such as, for example, when heirs and beneficiaries clash; property named in the will cannot be found; a "second will" appears; or the existence of estate real property in another state requires additional proceedings in that state to have the property lawfully transferred.

But not all estates are complicated, and not all are fraught with disputes and tough legal questions. The personal representative of a simple estate might be able to go it alone or proceed with limited attorney involvement.

So, what does a "simple will" in a "simple estate" look like? Most wills, even the complex, follow a generally accepted format. A "simple" will does not involve many special conditions and beneficiaries and will control assets that are easy to count and distribute. There will be sufficient assets to cover debts and satisfy the wishes of the testator. The following is a sample of a simple will:

LAST WILL AND TESTAMENT

OF

JOHN B. GOODE

I, John B. Goode, resident of the Town of Essex, County of Middevale, in the State of North State, being of sound mind and memory, and with understanding of all I possess, do hereby make, publish and declare this document to be my Last Will and Testament. I hereby revoke and declare null and void all Wills and Codicils previously made by me.

ARTICLE I: DECLARATIONS

I declare that I am married as of the date of this Will and that my wife's name is Georgia B. Goode. I further declare that I have two (2) adult children, namely: Cory B. Goode, my son, of Jordanville, South State, and Marlana Z. Goode-Barre of Hindville, South State.

ARTICLE II: DEBTS, EXPENSES, AND TAXES

I direct my Executrix to pay all of my legally enforceable debts, funeral expenses, and estate administration expenses as soon after my death as may be practicable, except that any debt or expense secured by a mortgage, pledge, or similar encumbrance on property owned by me at my death need not be paid by my estate, because there is mortgage insurance in place to cover all such encumbrances. Said mortgage insurance policies are kept with this Will to be sure there is no confusion on this point. I further direct that my Executrix shall pay out of residuary estate all taxes (together with interest and penalties thereon, if any) assessed upon my estate, or upon any property included as part of my gross estate, whether such property passes under the provisions of this Will or otherwise.

ARTICLE III: SPECIFIC BEQUESTS

A. I bequeath my coin collection to my son Cory B. Goode if he survives me by thirty (30) days. If Cory does not survive me by thirty (30) days, I bequeath the coin collection to Cory's son, Michael J. Goode, my grandson. If Michael J. Goode also does not survive me by thirty (30) days, this coin collection bequest shall lapse and become part of my residuary estate.

B. I give and bequeath my gun collection to my daughter Marlana Z. Goode-Barre. If Marlana does not survive me by thirty (30) days, I bequeath the gun collection my grandson, Michael J. Goode. If Michael J. Goode also does not survive me by thirty (30) days, the coin collection bequest shall lapse and become part of my residuary estate.

ARTICLE IV: GENERAL BEQUEST

I give and bequeath the sum of $10,000.00 to my sister, Clovis Morris (nee Goode) of Essex, Middevale County, North State, if she survives me by thirty (30) days. If my sister, Clovis Morris does not survive me by thirty (30) days, this bequest to her shall lapse and become a part of my residuary estate.

ARTICLE V: REAL ESTATE

I give and devise to my wife, Georgia B. Goode, absolutely and free of trust or conditions, all of my right, title, and interest in and to all real estate that is deemed and is part of my probate estate, whether I own such real estate separately, jointly with her, or others, together with all property or liability insurance policies relating to such real estate. If my wife, Georgia, does not survive me by thirty (30) days, such real estate shall become part of my residuary estate.

ARTICLE VI: RESIDUARY ESTATE

A. All the rest, residue, and remainder of the property that I may own at the time of my death, whether real, tangible, intangible, personal, or mixed, of whatever kind and nature and wherever situated, including all property that I may acquire or become entitled to after the execution of this Will, or other gifts made by this Will that fail for any reason, but excluding any property over or concerning which I may have any power of appointment (all hereinafter referred to as my "residuary estate"), I bequeath to my wife, Georgia B. Goode outright and free of all conditions, except that she survive me by thirty (30) days.

B. If my wife Georgia does not survive me by thirty (30) days, then I give, devise, and bequeath my residuary estate, in equal shares, to my children who survive me and the surviving descendants of any of my deceased children, *per stirpes*, outright and free of conditions.

C. If none of my children or their descendants survive me, then I bequeath my residuary estate to the Charitable Fund of North State, with its principal office in Charityville, County of Merit, North State, to be used for its general charitable purposes for the benefit of residents of North State.

ARTICLE VII: APPOINTMENT OF EXECUTRIX

A. I nominate and appoint my wife, Georgia B. Goode, as Executrix of my estate under the directions of this Will. I repose my special trust and faith in her, direct that no bond or other security be required for the faithful performance of her duties or, if bond is required by the Court, that sureties thereon be waived.

B. If my wife, Georgia B. Goode, predeceases me or fails to qualify as Executrix or, having qualified, should die, resign, or become incapacitated, then I nominate and appoint my sister, Clovis Morris, as Executrix, and give her the same powers and authority as my original Executrix was given.

C. If my sister, Clovis Morris, predeceases me or fails to qualify as Executrix or, having qualified, should die, resign, or become incapacitated, then I nominate and appoint my attorney, Chelsea Smart, as Executrix, and give her the same powers and authority as my original Executrix was given.

D. In addition to any other powers that my be conferred by law, I give my Executrix under this Will, including any successor or successors thereto, those powers set forth in the North State General Statutes, any of which may be exercised without the need for court order

ARTICLE VIII: DETERMINATION OF CHILDREN AND DESCENDANTS

As used in this Will, the words "children," "descendants," and "issue" shall include children in gestation and legally adopted individuals and the descendants of legally adopted individuals, provided such adoption took place at the time the individual adopted was a minor in the jurisdiction in which the adoption took place.

ARTICLE IX: AFTER-BORN CHILDREN

If subsequent to the execution of this Will there shall be an additional child or children born to or adopted by me, I direct that such birth or adoption shall not revoke this Will and that all references herein to my children and their issue shall include both my present children and their issue and any such after-born children and their issue.

ARTICLE X: FORFEITURE PROVISION

If any beneficiary named in this Will contests the admission of this Will into probate, contests the appointment of Executrix, or institutes or joins in any proceedings as a plaintiff to contest the validity of this Will or any provision hereof (except in good faith and with probable cause), then all bequests in this Will to such beneficiary shall lapse and my estate shall be administered and distributed in all respects as though such beneficiary had not survived me.

IN WITNESS WHEREOF, I have subscribed my name to this, my Last Will and Testament, consisting of _____ pages; and, for purposes of identification, I have initialed each preceding page in the presence of two persons, signed below as my witnesses.

_____

John B. Goode

Signed, and declared by the above-named John B. Goode, in our joint presence, that this document his Last Will and Testament, and in his presence and in the presence of each other we each have signed our names hereon as witnesses on the day and year last above written, being of lawful age and competent to do so.

_____ of _____

_____ of _____

Last Will and Testament
of

VICTOR L. QUEST

I, VICTOR L. QUEST , a resident of the County of Taz
and State of Illinois, being of sound and disposing mind an
memory, do hereby make, publish and declare this to be my
will and testament, hereby revoking any other wills or c
heretofore made by me.

SECTION ONE

I hereby direct that all funeral expenses and
of administering my estate, and all estate, inheri
and succession taxes which become due by reason
be paid as soon as practicable after my death.
of my estate any right to recovery from any p

I direct that no security o
of my mother or my father be

I give the Executor

in each case to be exer

(a) To sell at
to borrow money and f
all or part of the r

The Goode sample will illustrates the basic provisions one expects to find in a Last Will and Testament. The Testator declares he is of sound mind and knows what he possesses. This legal recitation is considered important because it shows clearly that the writer of the document *intends* it to be a valid will, as opposed to a diary entry, plans for the future, or a mere list. Also important is the statement of where the will is made, as that triggers the laws of which state apply to the will.

Then Mr. Goode provides his basic instructions: pay debts, expenses, and taxes, and how to do it from the estate. From there, he instructs how the rest of his estate shall be distributed. Most of the estate goes to his wife if she survives him. He has specific bequests for his children, and a general bequest for his sister. The difference between specific and general bequests is the uniqueness of the bequest. A coin collection, a gun collection, Aunt Martha's Ming vase, a portrait of Uncle Amberville — these are specific items, that, while they might have saleable value, are unique pieces or collection of pieces. A general bequest of cash is not unique in the same sense; cash is already liquid. One dollar bill is the same as another. If parts of an estate have to be liquidated to pay bills because there is not enough money in it to satisfy all the distributions the testator desired, the last things that can be liquidated are specific bequests. The general undefined property of residuary clause goes first, then general bequests.

Even with simple wills, disputes can arise, though. The heirs and beneficiaries do not always agree on what belonged to the testator and therefore, rightfully is part of the estate. A personal representative may have to grapple with a family member's assertion of ownership of an item that is bequeathed to someone else in the will or deeded to the testator before his death. Such situations cannot always be resolved without the assistance of the court. The next case study is an example.

CASE STUDY:
THE ESTATE OF LASSMANN

Handling an estate can involve many tasks for the personal representative, from the routine to even the slightly bizarre. An example is the *Estate of Lassmann* in Waukesha County, Wisconsin.

Clifford Lassmann died on August 19, 2007, at age 67, when a horse boarded at his Sundrift Stables trampled him. In his will, Mr. Lassmann left all his worldly possessions to his best friend, Jackie Vogel. He also named Ms. Vogel as executrix of his estate.

Mr. Lassmann was survived by two adult daughters, to whom he had left nothing in his will. However, one of these daughters would inherit if Ms. Vogel failed to survive him by 30 days. This daughter sued the estate, contesting ownership of the purebred registered Morgan gelding, Sundrift City Slicker aka "Iggy," a champion show horse. Ms. Vogel had Iggy up for sale as an asset of the estate, while the daughter claimed Iggy belonged to her. Ms. Vogel produced an undated transfer agreement from the estate's papers, purporting to show that the daughter had signed Iggy over to her father before Mr. Lassmann died. The daughter contested this. A further problem was that the ownership transfer to Mr. Lassmann had not been recorded with the American Morgan Horse Association Registry.

The argument between Ms. Vogel, as executrix of the estate, and the daughter was referred to mediation by the probate court. Sadly, before these proceedings concluded, Iggy died. The court eventually decided in favor of Mr. Lassman's daughter, awarding her Iggy's ashes, his tail, and $50,000 cash from other assets of the estate.

This case shows how the personal representative might have personal interests that parallel formal fiduciary duties. Ms. Vogel was the beneficiary of the estate and thus had a personal interest in the fate of Iggy. Nevertheless, it was also her primary duty to protect an asset of the estate. As happened in this case, protecting the estate's interests might require court proceedings, appraisals (in this case the value of a pureblood horse), and verification of documents (the transfer of ownership of the horse). Thus, the personal representative's job can be a multidimensional process, which often requires a balancing of competing legal and family interests.

The *Lassmann Estate* case illustrates a situation in which legal assistance becomes necessary because there is a dispute that requires a court hearing over contested evidence — the legality of a document. The testator, Mr. Lassmann, had disinherited adult children and left everything to a person unrelated by blood. This is absolutely legal and was his right to do. Although the laws generally prevent complete disinheritance of a surviving spouse, other relatives are not automatically protected from disinheritance. Such situations do not always create disputes, even though there may be unhappiness within the family as a result. Had there been no dispute in the *Lassmann Estate*, the proceedings would have been straightforward, with only one person inheriting all.

What is a Simple Estate?

A simple estate will have one clear, uncomplicated, lawfully executed will that directs disposition of the decedent's property. There will be few heirs to notify, and the property involved will be easily identified and itemized. The estate will be of insufficient value to trigger tax returns and tax payments. Though the estate value for this threshold varies among states that levy their own, $5,120,000 is the current federal tax exemption value.

Many states also have what is called a summary or informal proceeding for smaller estates, which shortens the time involved to close the estate and minimizes the number of forms and proceedings required by the court. This amount varies by state as well. *Appendix A of this book includes a chart listing the availability of such minimized procedure by state, and more information about informal proceedings can be found in Chapter 3.*

What am I getting myself into?

Handling a probate estate boils down to following directions of the court, using the correct forms and filing them on time, paying scrupulous attention to detail, and handling the people involved with sensitivity and diplomacy, from court personnel and creditors to heirs and beneficiaries of the deceased, and other third parties. Here is a basic outline of some of the things a simple estate encompasses:

Forms: Managing an estate is a matter of completing and organizing forms, principally the court forms used by your particular court. Many courts now have their forms online, so the Internet is the first place to look. Locate the court for the county of the decedent's main residence at the time of death. Check to see if the court has its forms and other useful information for you to review online. Read everything the court publishes online and print out the forms if they are provided.

Procedure: Not all courts have their materials on the Internet yet. If your court does, you have them and other information provided by the court at your fingertips. Otherwise, you can obtain the forms required by the court by making a visit to the court and asking for an information packet and copies of the forms the court uses for probating a will (or filing an estate without a will if no will exists). If you already have printed out materials from the court's online information, including forms, take these materials to the court and verify you have the correct information. Sometimes forms are changed and in use by the court before the Internet versions are updated. You want to have what the court requires. Court personnel will not give legal advice, but they can provide the forms and any informational brochures and other documents the court uses for administration of estates.

Attention to detail: Details are inherent in any form-driven process. Estate administration is definitely form-driven, but the details do not stop there. The forms reflect the culmination, the report, of the details you organize as part of the estate, such as: list of property items from tangible things to stocks, bonds, and bank accounts; list of heirs with addresses and phone numbers; list of beneficiaries in the will (which may not be all or any of the heirs) with addresses and phone numbers; correspondence with heirs, beneficiaries, banks, creditors, insurance representatives, and various others that have some business or attachment to the estate; and the decedent's records.

Meeting deadlines: Court filings, tax filings, and newspaper publication of notices have to be done at prescribed times during the estate administration. The court sets these deadlines. Some can be extended by application to the court in advance, but how much leeway you will have depends on the court and its policies.

Communication: The personal representative needs to keep in contact with family members, creditors, court personnel, and service providers in connection with management of the estate. Beneficiaries of the estate especially have a need to know what is going on.

Recordkeeping: Keeping track of documents and keeping them in order is one of the most important functions carried out by the personal representative. From the first collection and review of the decedent's papers to filing the final account and closing out the estate, the personal representative is dealing with documents, forms, correspondence, receipts, and other various records. Whether kept in a file cabinet or in computer files or both, these records are the personal representative's lifeblood. They are the means of organizing and discharging the duties of managing the estate and will prove, if necessary, that the personal representative properly carried out his or her fiduciary duties and obligations.

Is a Lawyer Required?

Technically? No. Two likely reasons most people would prefer to proceed without a lawyer in managing an estate are: (1) saving money and (2) saving time. Lawyers do not and should not work free. Probate procedure provides for the court to approve the attorney fees paid out for the lawyer's services, as well as the personal representative's fees. Unless the personal representative has chosen to waive his or her fees, a lawyer's involvement means double fees will be paid out of the estate's assets for the estate's management. With the exception of the higher priority court costs, taxes, and funeral costs, the personal representative's and attorney's fees generally have a higher priority than other debts and come out of the estate's assets before debts are paid and bequests distributed. How the personal representative and attorney fees are determined are set by state statute or court rule. Every state provides a formula for determining the amount of fees. These fees are scaled to the value of the estate and must be approved by the court before they can be paid. *A state-by-state listing of current provision for estate representative fees is included in Appendix A of this book.*

Proceeding without a lawyer can save time for the personal representative as well, because one less person is there with whom to meet and coordinate. Legal counsel simply cannot take over the personal representative's job. Rather, the personal representative provides legal counsel with the same information necessary to process the estate that he or she would be using to prepare the documents personally. To the extent the personal representative can handle the estate personally, time is streamlined, and he or she has the convenience of keeping his or her own schedule.

If an estate is small, with few assets and few complications, the personal representative should be able to traverse the procedure without a lawyer or with minimal professional assistance. It is a matter of becoming familiar with the local court's procedures and forms. With an understanding of the process, an informed decision about use of legal counsel can be made.

Common mistakes of lay people in representing estates

Even if the estate is simple and small, you, as the personal representative, must be careful to follow all the rules and laws of the court to ensure you perform your tasks so the estate is handled in a legal and binding manner. This is possible; however, the following are examples of the types of mistakes that can occur in the course of handling even a simple estate. Some problems are easily remedied and just cause time delays, while others are more serious.

- *Failure to get a sufficient number of certified death certificates in the beginning:* Death certificates are needed for all manner of communications, such as: court filing of the will and for appointment as estate representative or filing an intestate

estate, insurance companies for policy payouts, financial institutions to close out (or open) accounts, creditors who have accounts to be paid and closed, switching over utilities on real estate, federal government for Internal Revenue Service, Social Security Administration, Veterans Administration, other taxing authorities, real estate transfers, and vehicle transfers. If several of the foregoing are likely to be involved, start with at least a dozen death certificates. It takes time to get more. Some places will accept copies; others require original certified copies. If you start out with only four to six certified death certificates, as is commonly done, you are likely to come up short at an inopportune time.

- *Failure to scrupulously read the decedent's mail* — including items that look like "junk mail" — to be sure insurance policies, legal notices, financial papers, bills, checks, etc. are not missed. Sizable checks payable to the decedent have been thrown away as junk mail in some cases. These were not discovered until much later after an estate was closed, which raised tax problems, implications for filing an incorrect estate inventory, and additional distribution of estate assets.

- *Failure to discover bank accounts or safety deposit boxes:* Every bank where the decedent had an account should be queried about safety deposit boxes. Similarly, overlooking keys that are clearly safety deposit box keys can leave a box undiscovered, especially if that was the only service the decedent had at that bank. When you are appointed as personal representative, you can send a form letter with a copy of your appointment papers (often called "letters of authority") from the court and a photocopy of the death certificate to every bank in the area and ask if the decedent had any accounts or safety deposit boxes with the bank. Also, if the decedent was computer-active, it is important to review his or her computer records for online bank accounts. Most banks will accept a copy of the personal representative's appointment papers and the death certificate, but some might require certified ones.

• *Failure to file decedent's final personal income tax return if required:* Depending on the date of death, the decedent might have one or two income tax returns to file with federal and state, and possibly local, tax authorities. Death early in a year raises the question of whether the decedent's previous year's tax return was filed yet. A return for the year in which the decedent died also usually has to be prepared and filed. (An exception would be a case where the decedent had insufficient income to require a tax filing.) In addition to the legal filing requirement, it is possible the estate will have a tax refund coming, or tax owed that must be paid.

• *Accept and spend decedent's last Social Security check without checking to see if the funds are due back to the government:* Most people now have their monthly Social Security income paid by direct deposit into a bank account. Make sure the federal government is not owed back the last deposited payment, which might come in before notice of death is processed.

• *Failure to check the name in which real property insurance is held and transfer it with the insurance company:* In many states real property insurance cannot lawfully be held in a deceased person's name. The assets of the estate must be insured, which protects you in your fiduciary capacity as well as the assets themselves. If the decedent owned property in his or her name that becomes part of the probate estate, checking on insurance should be one of the first things you do. The estate needs to become the insured party, not the decedent. Find out who is decedent's insurance agent and call him or her to discuss the status of the insurance. You do not have to keep the insurance with this agent if you feel you can do better with another agency, but that is the place to start and it might be easier to maintain continuity of agent and coverage for the short term. This is one of the places that likely will require a certified death certificate and your certified court papers appointing you as the estate representative.

- *Overlook a claim owed to the estate:* Money owed to the decedent at time of death becomes money owed to the estate unless a contractual provision says the obligation is extinguished with the death of the decedent. One such overlooked claim is arrearage of child support or alimony. The personal representative needs to attempt to collect the arrearage.

Many such potential errors are avoided easily by knowledge, careful organization, and preparation for handling the estate. If the job is overwhelming to you though, or obvious complications threaten to make the job too complex for you to handle alone, legal assistance might be prudent and even necessary.

When a lawyer's services are advisable

Certainly legal questions cannot be discounted. Legal advice obtained early in the process might head off complications and forestall the need for prolonged disputes. Any complicated situation raised by the estate should be posed to legal counsel. A lawyer can be retained at any stage of the probate proceedings, for a limited purpose or to take on the entire process, so do not hesitate to start the process yourself. You always can call on the services of a lawyer if you get in over your head. The following kinds of issues should warrant the help of a lawyer.

Any question about the will's validity: For example, you have what you believed to be the decedent's valid will, but then a copy of another will is found. This raises a legal issue for which an attorney's counsel is advisable.

Potential disputes by surviving heirs: For example, the will expressly disinherits or fails to name a surviving spouse or a stranger appears who claims to be a long lost child of the deceased (who also is not named in the will). Another troublesome situation might be a beneficiary's dispute with how estate property is being divided, sold, or disbursed. Disputes among or by heirs against the estate might involve legal proceedings in the probate court, including hearings, for resolution by the court. *Estate of Lassman* in the case study above is an example of just such a situation. Legal counsel's assistance in these proceedings will be important for the best interest of the estate and might even be required by the court.

Dispute about your appointment: An angry beneficiary of the will or an heir might challenge your appointment as the personal representative. Unless you wish to step aside, you should have assistance of legal counsel for this issue.

Complex financial matters: If the estate is large, with many properties or other large financial holdings involved, legal counsel is advisable to ensure compliance with all required tax filings and other legal issues. Additionally, an accountant's services likely will be necessary as well.

Legal proceedings against the estate: Just as a person or business can be sued, so can an estate. These should not be handled without the assistance of legal counsel.

Although several circumstances might require you to retain legal counsel, many estates are small and simple. The personal representative, who has the time and commitment and who is armed with knowledge, can handle most small estates. The process is not difficult when you understand it.

CASE STUDY: GETTING THROUGH PROBATE

Law Offices of James N. Reyer, P.A.
5301 North Federal Highway, Suite 130
Boca Raton, FL 33487
561-241-9003 — voice
561-988-9892 — fax

Probate is the process through which a person's assets pass to his or her beneficiaries at the time of death through the oversight and supervision of a court. The assets in a probate matter are those that a person held in his or her name alone and that do not automatically pass to the beneficiaries.

The court proceeding ensures that all assets are properly administered, that all beneficiaries receive their appropriate shares of the estate, and that all estate creditors are paid. A court will supervise the terms and conditions of the deceased person's last will and testament, or in the absence of a will, the statutory terms for the passing on of property at death. Probate can be a simple procedure in some states and a complex proceeding in others. The complexity of probate is also determined by the size of the estate, the number and type of assets, creditor claims, and the cooperation (or lack thereof) of the beneficiaries.

The best manner in which to handle probate is to hire competent legal representation to see you and the beneficiaries through the process. This is mandated by statute in some states, but it is always a sound practice. The most important thing to do during the administration of an estate is to properly identify the assets in the estate, clarify ownership, and disclose to all beneficiaries exactly how the process will transpire and when to expect a distribution.

Probate is not always necessary. Proper estate-planning techniques can avoid probate altogether through vehicles such as a revocable living trust or a life estate deed. In addition, if multiple people own assets (for example with a "joint tenancy with the right of survivorship" designation), upon the death of one owner, the surviving owner or owners will acquire title to the asset without the need for a legal process.

When a person dies without a will, the state he or she lives in has a will for him or her. This is legally called "intestacy." It is a common fallacy that when someone dies without a will, his or her assets pass to the state. This is not true. Every state has a statutory schedule of who inherits property if a person dies without a will. This results in close relatives taking ownership of the assets. Sometimes, this is not what the deceased person would have wished. Draft your estate-planning documents to reflect what you want, so that your beneficiaries will not have to rely on statutes. Close family members can, to some extent, modify the statutory distribution if they are entitled to shares and do not want to take them. Put your wishes on paper as prepared by a competent estate-planning attorney.

Chapter 2

The Personal Representative

T he duties of a personal representative need not be viewed as drudgery. It is an important service. Whether named by the deceased in the will or called into service by the court, the personal representative's appointment is an honorable service of loyalty and trust, known as a fiduciary duty. Usually a relative or friend of the deceased, the personal representative performs a final service for someone who was close.

Even though it is a big responsibility, you would benefit from being named the personal representative of a loved one's estate in several ways. You have the opportunity to do one last good deed for your close friend or relative, that is, making sure his or her last wishes are carried out exactly as he or she wanted. You also gain valuable insight into the legal estate process that then can be used to make sure your own estate is as planned and official as possible. You also get a modest fee from the estate for performing these services, though this fee can be waived if that is your wish. *This monetary compensation will be covered in more detail at the end of the chapter.* Regardless of your reasons, being a personal representative, even in a trying time, can be a fulfilling and worthwhile pursuit.

Understanding the "Legalese"

Many archaic terms still abound in the probate world. These words have come down through hundreds of years of the law's development. The specific wording related to probate matters might differ slightly among the various states, each of which has its own origin in the history of the court system.

As you now know, "personal representative" is the general term that refers to a person appointed to represent the estate of a deceased person. By definition, the personal representative's responsibilities do not arise until the death of the person whose affairs are at issue. In this case, the personal representative's responsibilities will be limited to the length of time it takes to handle the affairs of the estate through the probate process. Other terms for this person are used in the various states. For example, Louisiana calls an estate a "succession" and, therefore, often refers to the personal representative as the "succession representative."

If the personal representative is appointed by will, a man is termed the *executor* of the estate, and a woman the *executrix*. These words come from the deceased having appointed whom he or she wishes to "execute" the instructions provided in the will, that is, according to the way the deceased — the *testator* — wanted it to be done. The court recognizes the testator's choice of personal representative and makes the appointment official.

Sometimes, the person named in a will cannot serve or does not wish to serve. No one can be "made" to serve. In such cases, or in cases where no will expresses the testator's wishes, the court will have to appoint someone else the personal representative. In this case, the court's appointed estate representative is called an *"administrator"* if a man, or *"administratrix"* if a woman. In many states, when a personal representative has to be replaced before an estate is completed, the new replacement representative is called an *"administrator (or administratrix) de bonis non."* De bonis non is Latin for "assets not yet administered." Thus, the replacement representative *de bonis non* is necessary to handle those assets not yet administered in the estate.

The personal representative of an estate is a *fiduciary*, which means a person who has the power and control over the money and property of another person or group of persons. This is a position requiring loyalty, honesty, and trust. For this reason, the law requires a fiduciary to use reasonable care at all times to protect the assets entrusted to him or her and to act in the best interest of their owner. In an estate, the personal representative's fiduciary duty covers the assets and affairs of the deceased and includes a duty owed to the estate beneficiaries to the extent of their interest in the estate. The personal representative also is considered an officer of the court where the estate is filed in probate because the personal representative performs his or her duties under the rules of the court, the law of the state, and the court's orders about the estate.

Other legal roles you could play

You could be asked to take on other fiduciary roles in addition to being a personal representative of an estate. In planning for the estate, the decedent also might set up a trust and name you as the trustee. As a trustee, you would have separate stand-alone fiduciary duties.

A "trustee" is responsible for the management of a trust set up by a person (the trustor or grantor) who has established a sum of money and/or other property of value (the trust *res*) to be handled for the benefit of someone else (the trust beneficiary). The trust might be effective during the trustor's lifetime or might not take effect until the trustor dies, depending on the terms and purpose of the trust. A trust is a stand-alone legal entity that continues until it is terminated either by its terms or by law. The management of a trust could last for many years, depending on its terms. Therefore, a trustee's service can last much longer than the term of a personal representative of an estate. The trustor also can set up a trust for the trustee, or the trustor can be the beneficiary of the trust during his lifetime. The trustor might designate his successor in his will or set it up in the trust terms. *Chapter 7 of this book explains more about trusts.*

The testator also might name you as a *guardian* or *co-guardian* of a minor child or disabled adult who is a beneficiary of the estate. Some states use the term *"conservator"* for this specific type of fiduciary responsibility. A guardian has the legal responsibility, conferred by a court, to look after the affairs and welfare of another person. This also is an independent role, one that lasts until the child reaches age of majority (age 18) or for the lifetime of a disabled person. As with other fiduciary positions, if you cannot take this on or cannot continue to perform this responsibility for any reason for the needed duration, then someone else will be appointed in your place.

It is not unusual for the same person to serve in these multiple capacities. Also, more than one person can be appointed to serve concurrently in these roles. For example, a testator can appoint two or more persons to serve jointly as executors of an estate. Similarly, more than one person can serve together as guardians and trustees. In these cases, they have equal fiduciary responsibility, plus the responsibility to work together. If a dispute arises among co-representatives that cannot be resolved, the court will have to step in to make the decision. Because multiple representatives in disagreement could slow down the estate proceedings, testators often do not appoint more than one person to serve at the same time. If it is done, it is usually in situations where an estate is complex or the testator wants two or more persons involved together for family reasons.

CASE STUDY:
A SIMPLE EXAMPLE

Bob Lee*
*Names have been changed for the
contributor's privacy and protection

When my mother died, my brother and I went through the normal bereavement process, which just about everyone must face at a certain time in life. Still, despite the grieving period and emotions involved, we had to face that property and assets had to be formally distributed. This was not a problem, I thought. Frankly, it was the last thing on my mind. Dealing with my mother's death was the center of everything. Changing the names on the property title would be something routine. I remember calling the local county clerk's office and explaining the situation. My mother had passed away, and we had to change the name on papers, so tax statements could be sent to the right person. I knew that our state law said that my brother and I each would get half, and there was no conflict between us. So, I thought, just send over the paperwork, and we will sign.

I was naïve enough to believe everything could be done over the phone in a few minutes and verified in a few days. It was then that I heard the person on the other end of the line mention "probate," a word that sounded familiar but foreign. The property would have to go through the probate court, she explained. Probate is a court procedure through which assets of the deceased are passed to his or her beneficiaries under the state court's supervision according to state law. The court's role is to assure that the assets are properly administered, all beneficiaries receive share of the estate and all creditors of the estate are paid.

My brother agreed to my appointment as personal representative for the estate. In a few months, with legal assistance, probate was completed and title to my mother's property was transferred to my brother and me.

Handling my mother's estate was relatively simple. However, no one estate is the same as another. Each personal representative has specific duties and responsibilities. There may be just one property to deal with, or there may be several different types to disburse to a variety of beneficiaries. The collection and payment of debts, calculating taxes, filing of forms, inventorying and appraising assets, handling the deceased's final affairs, and arranging details of all other matters of an estate differ for every personal representative.

The same is true for the trustee, who handles a property similar to the probate estate. The difference is the property is confined within the terms of a trust. The trustee must follow the trust agreement, a governing document made by the creator of the trust. The trust's creator sets up guidelines for the holding, management, and investment of the trust assets and directs who shall receive income and assets from the trust (the trust beneficiaries), and how income from the trust will be paid out. The trustee holds the legal title to the trust property until the terms of the trust are completed.

The personal representative of an estate is entrusted with the management of property and always will be acting on the behalf of the estate. The personal representative must know how to deal with grief-stricken and sometimes angry beneficiaries and fully understand the time and effort involved before taking on the important job. It may be as simple as handling the decedent's wishes or as complex as settling quarrels among relatives involved in business transactions. The estate's personal representative will be organizing assets, paying debts, managing an entire estate, and interacting with the court and others until the process is completed.

In the above case study, the personal representative's mother had not left a will. In this situation, the deceased is said to be *intestate*. Mr. Lee and his brother understood their entitlement to her estate assets as her surviving children under state law, but the estate still needed a personal representative. In the absence of a will, the court appointed the personal representative. This could have been a family member of the decedent, an attorney, or a friend or business associate of the decedent. In Mr. Lee's case, the court appointed one of the two adult surviving children. This is the normal approach. The two brothers agreed on the appointment, and it may have been more convenient for one than the other. If they were not in agreement, they would have had to present their dispute to the court as to whom should be appointed, and the court would have made its decision accordingly.

The court would consider such factors as which brother lived closer to the court, had more familiarity with the estate matters, and otherwise made the most persuasive argument to be appointed. Sometimes the court will appoint co-representatives of an estate. Because this requires dual signatures to estate documents and the coordination of two people to make decisions about the estate, this cumbersome arrangement is not often done, especially for straightforward, relatively simple estates or where no dispute on appointment of the personal representative exists. On the other hand, if the decedent appoints co-executors in the will, the court will not interfere with this decision unless a dispute about it is brought before the court for resolution.

Who Can Be the Personal Representative of an Estate?

The personal representative appointed to handle the estate must be "competent." Competency means the person is of lawful age and has the sufficient mental faculties to handle the estate's business. For example, a person adjudicated to be mentally incompetent and under the care of a guardian would not be competent to serve as an estate's personal representative. A court might not deem someone who is seriously ill and bedridden competent.

Unless such an adjudication of incompetency exists, any adult (age 18 or over) who is a U.S. resident can be deemed competent to serve as an estate's personal representative, as can an institution such as a bank. State law in some states might impose other limitations, though. For example, some states limit appointment of personal representatives to in-state residents or disqualify someone who has been convicted of a felony. Whether a person is competent for the job of personal representative is ultimately the probate court's final determination. *A table of each state's minimal requirements for the personal representative is included in Appendix A of this book.*

The beneficiaries of an estate might contest who is to be appointed as the estate representative, though their wishes will not override the provisions of a will unless they can show good cause to convince a court that the testator's choice is unfit to serve.

To prove unfitness, they would have to show that the personal representative either does not meet the state law requirements to serve (e.g. age, residency) or is mentally incompetent to act as a representative. In some cases, a disgruntled family member might try to show that the personal representative has a conflicting personal interest in the estate. A personal representative, though, also can be a beneficiary of the estate, and often is, as, for example, when the deceased's surviving spouse is also the estate's personal representative. The key in such a situation is that the fiduciary responsibilities of the estate's personal representative override any interest the person has as someone who is also inheriting part of the estate. The estate property must be handled according to the directions of the will and the law, creditors must be paid, and taxes must be filed and paid. Any of these obligations could reduce the personal representative's own inheritance if the estate assets are not enough to cover all the obligations fully.

Bond requirements

Additionally, probate law in the various states requires that estate representatives post a bond with the court in a specified amount of money, such as equal to (or more) the estimated gross value of the estate's assets. A bond is like an insurance policy and is usually purchased with the help of the personal representative's own personal insurance provider. If your insurance company does not do this, your insurance agent can refer you to a company that does. Getting a bond or insurance policy does require a fee, similar to a premium paid for an insurance policy. This cost can be charged to the estate as an expense, but the personal representative will likely have to pay for it initially and apply for reimbursement from the estate after the court issues the appointment.

The reason for a bond requirement is to ensure the estate is protected if the representative, who holds the estate's assets within his or her fiduciary power, breaches that fiduciary duty and absconds with or willfully wastes the estate's funds. The testator might state in the will that the bond requirement is waived, and in many cases, the bond may be waived even if the testator does not specify a waived bond. Whenever the bond is not waived, though, or when the court requires it for some reason regardless of the will's provisions, a person who is unable to meet the bond requirement will not be able to serve as the estate representative. Rarely does this happen. A bond is not difficult to purchase through an insurance or bonding company. To avoid the hassle and expense to the estate of this extra step in the representative's appointment process, most testators expressly write in their wills that a bond shall not be required. If a bond is required and the process makes you uncomfortable for any reason, you do not have to accept the appointment.

How is a Person Selected?

As mentioned, the personal representative is usually someone known and trusted by the testator. The testator will have his or her own reasons for choosing the personal representative, but certain basic qualities should be considered. A married testator typically names the spouse or an adult child. An unmarried testator might name a family member or a good friend. The testator chooses a friend or family member because these people are already in a position of trust; they have the testator's confidence. However, the testator also should consider that the person named is available and able to handle the responsibility. Similarly, if the court has to make the appointment, the appointing judge will want to be satisfied that the person selected will be able to meet the estate representative's fiduciary obligations. This is not a "title only" position.

More important, you, as the personal representative, should evaluate for yourself if you want to take on the task. It takes time. It is a responsibility. It has legal obligations. It is, in essence, a part-time job.

Qualities of the personal representative

In drafting a will, most testators will look to a spouse or another close adult relative to name as their executor or executrix. Often, this person will be a beneficiary of the estate as well. A beneficiary is more likely to waive fees for serving the estate. Of prime concern to the testator is that the executor or executrix will be someone trusted and interested in carrying out the testator's wishes. First, the personal representative must be able to put the testator's wishes ahead of his or her own. The personal representative must meet the state's requirements to serve which at minimum will be of adult age (18 or over) and mentally competent. Considering the tasks involved in administering an estate, and the duty owed to the estate, the following are desirable qualities and considerations for the personal representative.

1. **Knowledge and understanding of the testator and the estate:** Administering a person's estate means carrying out that person's wishes after he or she is gone. Understanding the testator's intent and having knowledge of the testator's life and business will be helpful. Ideally, the testator will approach you during his or her lifetime to discuss the appointment, familiarize you with information about the estate, and answer any questions you might have. If this did not happen, study the terms of the will and assess the scope of what will be required to handle the estate before accepting the appointment.

2. **Organization and attention to detail:** Managing even a simple estate requires skill in organization and attention to detail. Categories of personal, family, property, and financial matters must be organized and handled for the estate. The probate process and tax laws, as applicable, will require calendar deadlines to be met.

3. **Patience, compassion, and good communication skills:** The personal representative must deal with family members who are grieving and maybe squabbling. They might not be happy with the personal representative's appointment, the testator's will provisions, or the reality of probate law and procedures. They might be difficult to find or reach. Others also might present a challenge, such as impatient creditors. Further, court personnel will be involved for filing of probate documents, such as banks and other institutions, and not all of them are easy to deal with. The personal representative will find that phone calls, email correspondence, and letters are routine and necessary parts of the job.

4. **Time:** Depending on the scope of the estate, the personal representative's tasks can be time-consuming, especially during the initial months of administration. If a person already has a full-time demanding job and family that leave little time for anything more to take on, the personal representative's role might not be advisable. It carries a fiduciary obligation with a legal responsibility that cannot be safely neglected.

A person lacking in time to devote to the required tasks of the personal representative, or in any of these necessary qualities, should consider declining the role. It is not a mandatory duty to accept the appointment of personal representative. If you feel that the job is going to require more time than you can set aside for it, that you are too emotionally invested in the situation to be objective, or that this simply is not something you want to do, then do not hesitate to decline the appointment.

When You Are Asked to Serve

You might learn of your appointment as an executor or executrix in a couple of ways. Ideally, the testator will have told you in advance and discussed his or her wishes with you, perhaps even giving you a copy of the will. Also, as the testator's spouse or close relatives, you might be the person who first finds and reads the will. If neither of these is the case, the person who has the will or the testator's attorney will contact you for probate of the will.

If no will exists, the testator's spouse or close relative files with the probate court to open the estate and appoint him or herself personal representative. According to court procedure, heirs of the testator are notified of the request for appointment as personal representative. They can agree (as in the Bob Lee case study above) or dispute. Sometimes, a surviving spouse or other close relative might approach another person, such as a close friend of the testator, to serve as a personal representative, in the belief this

person is better equipped for the job or will be a "neutral" person with whom all the heirs or beneficiaries can best get along.

If you are asked to serve as a personal representative, look at it as being offered a part-time job. Be prepared to schedule time on a regular basis to attend to estate matters. You also should set up space physically for keeping the estate records together, whether a file box, or dedicated file drawer. If you are used to working in a computer, set up a separate file folder for the estate, and keep your computer estate files together under that folder. If you share a computer with others, remember that your files are fiduciary and confidential. Therefore, either keep your estate records on a separate portable flash drive, or protect them in the computer hard drive with a password. Also, remember to back up your computer files on another separate drive.

Preparation is everything

The more guidance the testator has provided for his or her estate's personal representative, the easier the job will be. But such advance preparation does not always happen. Death itself is inevitable, but not its time. People do not always have time to plan beyond naming executors in their wills. Furthermore, death is not a favorite subject of conversation. This book provides information for the person suddenly thrust into the role.

Some people are organized and wish to provide information to their named representative before death. Do not discourage or avoid discussions about this information as seemingly "morbid." Welcome it. The discussion will make the testator feel more peaceful about having arranged his or her affairs, and the estate matters will be easier for you to manage because you have a previous understanding of the decedent's wishes. Ask the testator about provisions for heirs in the will. Is anyone being left out? If so, it will help you understand why. Is there property of special value such as a coin collection, classic car, or gun collection? Ask the testator if he or she has an appraisal list for these items and, if so, where the list is kept. Find out where the testator keeps these and other items of value and where he or she keeps tax and financial records. Does the testator have an attorney or accountant? If so, having the name and contact information for these people might be useful to you in managing the estate. Where is the original will kept? Does the testator wish you to keep the original or a copy of the will?

Things you should know

Before accepting the responsibility of the appointment, understand the scope of representation the estate will require. You will want to know if aspects about the people involved or the business of the estate itself are more than you wish to take on. Just because the estate is complicated, however, would not be in itself a reason to decline representation. A situation you perceive will be difficult might be manageable with assistance of legal counsel and/or other professional assistance, such as accountants, appraisers, and financial advisers. The point is to make an informed decision with an understanding of what will be involved. Ask, minimally, the following questions to get started:

Beneficiaries:
- Who are the estate's beneficiaries, and where are they located? Is there more than one beneficiary? If any beneficiaries are out of town, out of state, or out of the country, their distance is going to increase the difficulty of communicating with them and obtaining necessary agreements and signatures for the court process.

- If there is more than one beneficiary, what is the likelihood of disagreements between or among them? For example, the existence of a former spouse with children of the decedent raises such a potential issue. If one of the beneficiaries has been estranged from the family, the story relating to this might be a source of friction or animosity among the beneficiaries.

- Is there a surviving spouse? Has the surviving spouse been cut out of the will or been left less than the statutory entitlement? If so, the spouse has rights that come ahead of the will. Making sure these rights are lawfully protected will require additional forms and notices to be done as part of the court process. If the spouse elects to enforce these rights, which is called "taking against the will," then other beneficiaries' portions will be reduced to give the spouse his or her statutory entitlement.

- Are there surviving minor children? Does the estate provide for them? Are there guardianship issues of the minor children? Are any surviving children of contestable legal status as to inheritance, such as an illegitimate child or stepchild? Stepchildren do not have standing to inherit unless they are included by state statute. If the testator's will states that "all my children" are to receive something, stepchildren will not lawfully be included in the class of "children" unless the will has expressly defined "children" to include stepchildren. Illegitimate children who are not born within a marriage of the deceased will likely have inheritance rights under the law as included with the deceased's "children" unless the will has specifically excluded them.

- Are any heirs — named in the will or not — missing? This means time and effort to locate these people. Are there facts to suggest whether a missing heir should be presumed dead? Presumption of death laws vary by state, so you will need to know what your state requires in this situation for giving notice of the estate.

- Are there any heirs by law who are not named in the will? If so, they might contest it.

- Will satisfying debts owed by the estate mean spending money or liquidating property that was intended for beneficiaries? If so, the beneficiaries' entitlement will be reduced. How they are reduced and in what order depends on how the will covered this possibility or otherwise according to the priorities set up by your state's probate law.

The Will:
- Are there any issues about the will's validity? For example, is there any question regarding the testator's signature or the validity of the witnesses who signed the will? Was the will made out on the testator's deathbed? Has anyone raised a question about the testator's mental capacity to make a valid will?

- Do you have a copy of it? A copy is useful for reviewing what the will says, but only an original can be filed in court and followed for the estate. A copy will not come into play unless it can be proved the original is lost and the copy is a valid copy of the latest will to be accepted in its place.

- Is the original will readily available? A search must be done for the original will before it can be declared lost.

For example, a family member might remember that a will was prepared but have no knowledge about where the testator put the original.

- Does more than one purported will exist? Does the latest will fully replace the previous will or must the two wills be put together? Or, as another example, has a family member or other person come forward with another, later will that is alleged to be the true will intended by the testator?

- Can you locate the witnesses to the will if needed? Are they still living? If a will has to be validated in the probate court, or the testator's capacity is questioned at the time of signing the will, the witnesses' testimony will be necessary, if available, to confirm the circumstances, date, and testator's signature on the will.

- Are there codicils (amendments) to the will? If so, they must be validated the same as the will itself. A codicil changes the original will in some way, by reallocating property from one beneficiary to another, for example. Or, a codicil might change the executor or eliminate or add a beneficiary. The codicils and the will have to be read together to fully grasp how the estate is to be handled and distributed.

Real Property

- Is any real property covered by the will and therefore part of the probate estate? Is any of it out of state where it will be subject to ancillary proceedings of the other state for transfer? When property is situated in another state, and cannot be brought to you, as is the case with real estate and sometimes other types of property that is not easily moved or is titled in another state (e.g. vehicle, boat), a court action has to be filed in the other state to have the property transferred to the name of the beneficiary who has received it under the will or who has inherited it by law in the case of no will. A lawyer will need to be obtained in the other state to represent the estate in the local proceeding.

- Is there real property that the will directs to be sold, or which might have to be sold to pay debts of the estate? The property will need to be appraised and listed for sale. One consideration will be whether to go through a Realtor® or to sell the property directly to save the Realtor fees. The nature of the property, the market, the location of the property, its condition, and your available time to handle selling it are some of the factors you should consider in making this decision.

- Does the property generate rentals that will need to be collected by the estate during its pendency? For example, if the decedent owned a duplex rented out, and tenants are in residence, their rent will need to be paid to the estate until the property is transferred to its beneficiary or sold by the estate.

- Does the property require maintenance or repairs that must be done to keep its value and use before it can be transferred to its beneficiary or sold by the estate?

A qualified appraiser must appraise real property to determine its equivalent value as an estate asset as well as to set a price if it is to be sold. You will have to locate and hire an appraiser on behalf of the estate, and the estate pays the appraiser's fees. Some courts will require court approval of an appraiser or will have a court-approved appraiser list. Find out the court's requirements for using an approved appraiser before hiring an appraiser.

Non-probate Property

- Is there property you will have to account for as part of the taxable estate, even though it is not part of the probate estate? For example, the deceased and his daughter owned a three-acre lot under a joint and survivorship arrangement by which the lot automatically transferred to the daughter's name upon her father's death. This property transfers automatically by the survivorship deed provisions, so it is not part of the probate estate. However, the value of the decedent's interest, which is one-half the property's value, is includable in the taxable assets of the estate. Nearly all states have laws recognizing the option of transferring real estate outside of probate. It must be done by a properly drafted and executed joint survivorship deed prepared in accordance with state law.

Debts

- Are there sufficient assets to pay the estate debts? Will you have to have sales of property — liquidation — to acquire money to pay the debts?

- Are there debts that are contested? For example, a person claims the decedent owes him a sum of money and produces a promissory note signed by the decedent. The decedent's spouse, however, says that debt was paid off a long time ago, and the note was canceled; the note this person is showing you is not valid. It likely will take the court's action to resolve this dispute.

Assets

- Are there extensive assets? If the estate is valued more than $5.12 million, federal taxes are implicated, which require more work and hiring an accountant for the estate. Extensive assets also require a lot of time to list, evaluate, get appraised, and be responsible for during the time the estate is open.

- Are any assets missing or in dispute? For example, the will, made two years before the testator's death, states the decedent's gold necklace with the pavé diamond heart pendant is to be given to her daughter, Kay. The necklace cannot be found in the decedent's jewelry or among the rest of her possessions. Another daughter, Alice, is seen wearing the necklace to a relative's wedding. Alice claims her mother gave it to her six months before she died. Kay disputes this and says Alice must have taken it from their mother's bedroom after the funeral. In addition to the sum of money the necklace is worth, both daughters claim sentimental value for the necklace. If you cannot mediate an agreement between the two daughters on this that they both will sign, you will have to petition the court to resolve this dispute.

Taxes

- Is the estate large enough to trigger estate tax filings and payment obligations? Estates up to net value of $5.12 million beginning January 1, 2012, are exempt from federal estate tax. Estates over this amount are taxed at 35 percent. Unless Congress makes a change, as of January 1, 2013, the federal estate tax exemption will drop down to $1 million and the tax will increase to 55 percent. Your state also might have an estate tax separate from the federal tax. Some states have an inheritance tax. Some states, like Ohio, are in transition in changing their tax. Ohio has abolished its estate tax effective January 1, 2013. Because each state is different, you will need to find out what is required for your state and file the appropriate forms with tax payment out of estate funds, if the tax applies and is owed. *A chart in Appendix A of this book lists the current estate and inheritance tax requirements by state.* Keep in mind this area is in a state of nearly constant change.

- Are the decedent's records available to assist filing the final income tax returns? A personal income tax return usually must be filed for the decedent. Having the prior tax records for reference will make this task much easier. These records also should aid in determining income sources and property, such as bank accounts, stocks, and bonds, for the estate inventory.

Business Issues

- Did the decedent operate a business that is ongoing with the decedent's ownership in the business passed to the estate? Will the personal representative have interim obligations or duties with respect to the business operation? If so, this can become a complicated responsibility for which legal and accounting assistance will be important.

Ethical Will or Other Directives

- Did the testator leave any other writings or a video for guidance about his or her wishes for you and the family? These are not legally binding, but they often are helpful and can go far to prevent or resolve disputes.

The answers to these questions and others like them will help you decide if you have the time and fortitude to proceed with management of the estate. You might find you are not daunted by any of these questions once you know the answers because with knowledge, you are prepared and know how you will organize what needs to be done.

Compensation

Probate law provides that personal representatives will be compensated for their work. Each state has its own provision for how the personal representative's fees will be calculated. The state often will say "reasonable" compensation should be paid or that the personal representative receives fees equivalent to a certain percentage of the estate's assets. An example is Louisiana, which provides for both ways of calculating the personal representative's fees.

Louisiana says that the personal representative is to be paid a reasonable fee as stated in the will or, if there is no provision in the will, then as agreed by the estate's beneficiaries with the representative. If they cannot agree on what is reasonable, Louisiana law says then the fees will be 2.5 percent of the value of estate's inventory assets. So, in Louisiana, you can have a basic expectation of being paid 2.5 percent of the estate's value. If an estate is

valued at $100,000, the personal representative's fee can be ex-
pected to be at least $2,500 and possibly more if an additional
amount is deemed necessary to be "reasonable" for the work required by the estate. If the will provides a fee that is less than
$2,500, you would have a good argument in Louisiana that the
will does not provide for adequate and reasonable compensation
and that the court should allow for more. Whether "reasonable"
fees or the 2.5 percent of the estate applies, the court in both cases
can increase the basic compensation if the personal representative applies for it and can show that the additional compensation
is justified by the work and time the estate required. Thus, while
the $2,500 is a good guideline in this case, fees could end up be-
ing more if the court agrees.

The courts have such discretion in most states. For this reason,
as well as proving you are carrying out your fiduciary duties appropriately, keep track of your time spent on estate matters and
costs expended for reimbursement carefully. Use a time sheet for
yourself, such as the following form, and keep it as part of your
estate file records. You can do this with the time sheet in a note-
book in hard copy or as a running document in your computer.
Some examples of hypothetical time entries are included here to
illustrate. *A copy of this form for your use is also included in Appendix
B of this book and on the CD-ROM.*

Sample Time Sheet and Expenses, Estate Personal Representative

Date	Description of Work Done	Total Time Spent (in tenths of an hour)	Expenses Avanced or Incurred	Comment & Follow-up
Dec. 12, 2012	Visited courthouse to speak with clerk of court, check the forms required, filing fees, and obtain court forms. Filled out Forms to file the Will and get appointed	4.5	Mileage = 30 miles Parking = $5.00	Courthouse opens at 8 a.m. closes at 4:30 p.m. Except 4 p.m. on Fridays Cannot take cell phone into courthouse File forms tomorrow (Dec. 13)
Dec. 13, 2012	File forms at courthouse, advanced filing fee	1.8	Mileage = 30 miles Parking= $4.00 Filing Fee $100.00	Go back to pick up certified letters of authority on Friday.
Dec. 14, 2012	Took 1st Inventory of Bill's (decedent) house.	4	Mileage = 10 miles	Located, marked everything listed in will. Got all keys to the house; should change locks; no idea how many keys are around.
Dec. 14, 2012	Telephone call with Deadbolt Doug's Lock Services to have Bill's house locks changed — 866-5555; DOUG; spoke with Doug Doright, owner; he knew Bill from Rotary	0.3		Will meet Doug at house 9 a.m. tomorrow, Dec.15; Doug running this on account until I am set up to pay from estate.
Dec. 14, 2012	Telephone call with Jodi James, Bill's niece, about house-sitting Bill's house Jodi's cell — 700-555-1234	0.5		She will stay in house and house-sit for at least 3 months if needed; will meet her at house 9 a.m. tomorrow, Dec. 15, and she can go over everything and get new key. She agreed to $100.00/month house-sitting fee.

The testator might state in the will that the personal representative shall serve without compensation. This is not binding on a personal representative. A personal representative can decline to serve under these circumstances.

On the other hand, a personal representative can refuse to take compensation. The latter is often the case where the personal representative is also the sole beneficiary of the estate. The personal representative's compensation comes out of the estate's proceeds before the beneficiaries receive the final distribution to which they are entitled. If the personal representative will receive the entire distribution, he or she defers to the inheritance rather than take fees that are taxable income.

CASE STUDY: A LOVED ONE'S EXPERIENCE

Zelda Morgan
Dallas, Texas

Zelda Morgan had a good experience with her siblings and with the entire will and estate business when her mother died recently. She had been chosen as both sole executor and power of attorney for her mother before she died. Thrust into the situation, Morgan knew that she and her mother had never had a problem talking about their wishes after death and her siblings (there were two) did not try to override her or give her a hard time.

"Even though I was the youngest, my brother and sister knew my mother wanted me as her executor and power of attorney, and they didn't try to butt into me doing my job in those roles. Because we all got along, which is apparently not so common, I involved them every step of the way so we all three could feel like we were making the decisions together, and we really were."

Even before Morgan's mother died, she knew her mother did not want to be hooked up to a machine keeping her alive. Morgan also knew that someday she would have to be the one to make that call; when it happened, it was not what she expected.

Morgan's mother was 82 years old, so it was not uncommon for her to have to go to the hospital for various health reasons. On this day, she had been taken to the hospital, and Morgan had been called to come there as her power of attorney. She found her mom in the emergency room, and the nurse in charge told her that her mother would be able to see her and would regain consciousness in about 30 minutes. Thirty minutes later, she was called to the ICU with her husband and brother and asked if her mother had wanted to be on life support.

"I had no idea what a life support machine even looked like before that day," Morgan recalled. "The doctor called me in the room and asked me if my mother wanted to be on life support. I asked him what he was talking about. Unfortunately, this doctor had the bedside manner of a baboon, and when I asked him if my mom would wake up, he shook his and said, 'Nope, she's out of it.' She was like a limp dishrag. After a few choice words with the doctor, we called the family and told them to come. Two hours later my mom died, but with her siblings, children, and friends by her side."

Morgan's father had died in March 2005, and it was at that time that her mother began preparing for what would happen in the event of her death. Fortunately, she had all the paperwork together as well as let her children know where the money was, how much there was, and any of the other details that would be necessary after she passed away. It was at this time that Morgan's mother also put her in charge.

"My brother and his wife also moved in with my mom; this way, she was able to live at home until she died. So my brother took care of the day-to-day, my sister handled any phone calls relating to insurance or business matters, and I made the overall bigger decisions. Everyone got to take part in my mother's last days," Morgan said.

When her mother died, Morgan had a copy of the will and most of the funeral expenses had been paid for already. Her mother had also paid all her bills off with the exception of one credit card, and she had supplemental insurance, leaving no hospital or medical bills that had to be paid.

"I have never heard of anyone doing it, and I can't believe how well my mother took care of matters before she died — she left us quite a bit of money and no problems. I also think because of this, my siblings and I got along so well because we knew my parents would have been horrified if we had argued."

Probate Procedure

his chapter outlines the procedural steps of administering an estate. Bear in mind that variances exist in specific states, but the following is the order of procedure for administering a simple estate.

Remember to keep meticulous records of everything you do with the estate, even if you have assistance from an attorney. Document everything you do, and keep the records filed in an orderly fashion. This will provide evidence you have discharged your fiduciary obligations properly and lawfully as the estate's personal representative. This also will provide valuable information should any questions arise about the estate, whether during its pendency or after it is closed.

Start at the Beginning

Your first steps when starting out this process are to locate the will and obtain death certificates of the deceased so you can begin transferring all powers to yourself. The will is of utmost importance because it defines the type of estate to be filed and those who inherit. Without a will, the process is defined by statute.

Find the will

If you do not have it already, obtain the original will. A search of the decedent's personal papers should be done first. If the will is not found, you will need to conduct a wider search of possible locations. The decedent might have deposited the original will under seal with the court. This is an option in many states. Contact the court in the county of the decedent's last primary residence to see if this was done. If the decedent had moved residences across county or state lines during the past few years, you might need to check with the courts of prior residence.

Another possible location is the decedent's safety deposit box. Not all states permit immediate access to safety deposit boxes. If you are not able to enter the box for purpose of locating a will, you will need to file with the court without a will to get authorization to enter the box. If the decedent had a co-tenant on the box, that person should be able to access the box on his or her own authority.

The decedent might have deposited the original will with his or her lawyer. If the decedent's lawyer should prove to be unknown, contact the local bar association for assistance in seeking out the decedent's lawyer.

Obtain death certificates

Obtain several certified copies of the death certificate. The county where death occurred issues the death certificate; the funeral home will provide the initial copies with their cost included on the funeral bill. The funeral provider might ask how many certificates are desired. The cost of the death certificates (which can range from $5 to $25 per official certified copy, depending on the state agency) is a cost paid by the estate. As mentioned in Chapter 1, if you foresee needing to speak to many different entities, a dozen death certificates probably would cover all needs. However, if you want to be more precise, follow these instructions:

The death certificates will be needed for your initial filing with the court, tax returns, banks, and other institutions that have the decedent's accounts. These include life insurance policies, Social Security Administration paperwork, government agencies that might be involved with title transfers (e.g. bureau of motor vehicles, county recorder of real estate deeds and deed transfers, out-of-state courts that might become involved for real estate transfer or other ancillary estate matters, other out-of-state agencies that might become involved or needed for property transfers), utility companies (if death certificate is required to transfer utilities on real property). Do a quick assessment of the likely areas where a death certificate will be required and assume you will need at least two more than you estimate. Although additional death certificates always can be obtained, it takes time to do so. It is best to have them when needed.

Filing with the court

The first decision is whether an estate needs to be filed at all. If the decedent has no appreciable probate property or debts, it might not be necessary to file anything, even if there was a will. Here is an example:

Uncle Jim just died of a heart attack. Several years ago, Uncle Jim wrote a simple will leaving all his worldly possessions to his wife, Aunt Betty. He named Aunt Betty as his executrix in the will. However, at the time of Uncle Jim's death, he and Aunt Betty own their real estate property by deed as joint owners with right of survivorship and their bank accounts in joint ownership with right of survivor arrangement as well. They have one car, and it is titled to Aunt Betty. Under their joint ownership arrangements, Uncle Jim's interest in the real estate and the bank accounts passes to Aunt Betty immediately and directly when he dies. These assets are not subject to probate. He does not own anything else except his clothing and a few miscellaneous items of no intrinsic value. He also did not have any debts separate from his marriage. There is a mortgage on the house but he had life insurance that will pay off most of it and also his insurance expenses. Uncle Jim's ownership interest in the non-probate property falls far short of the federal estate tax threshold, and there is no state estate or inheritance tax. In short, although there is a will, there is no property to probate under the will and no debts to pay under the will. There is no probate estate. If there is probate property, though, you will have to decide what kind of estate is required.

A simple estate might not need the full process. The first step is to determine what needs to be filed. Most courts provide for a summary process for small estates. This type of summary administration is like a "short form" estate that puts the process on a fast track. If there are few assets and a will, there is no need for the long, drawn-out process.

Summary probate procedure

A good example of summary probate is found in California, which allows four types of summary probate procedures to transfer property for small estates, with or without a will. These are:

- Personal property — 40 days after death if no other estate proceedings pending

- Real property that does not exceed value of $20,000 — six months after death if no other estate proceedings pending and funeral expenses, last illness bills, and unsecured debts are paid

- Combined real or personal property not exceeding $100,000 — 40 days after death, gross value of estate does not exceed (certain property excluded from valuation)

- Surviving spouse is entitled to the property.

In these situations, the transfer can be done by affidavit of the person entitled to the property in California. The process is further explained at **www.apeopleschoice.com** (select "Probate").

Check with your court in your state to determine if summary proceedings apply to your estate. Summary or informal shortened proceedings move much faster than "formal" proceedings, but specific periods are involved.

Steps for Filing a Formal Probate

If your state does not allow summary proceedings or if the estate you are managing is too complex to qualify for informal proceedings, you will need to file a formal probate with the court. The filing periods vary by state; check with the court for the filing times for your state.

Here are the steps you will need to take to file the estate officially:

1. *Initial court filing.* File your application to be appointed personal representative with the original will and death certificate, using the court's designated forms for this purpose. The initial filing includes the following information, supplied on the court forms:

   a. Request to admit will to probate

   b. Your request to be appointed personal representative and your information

   c. Information about the decedent (e.g., name, social security number, last primary address, date of birth, date of death)

   d. Certified copy of death certificate

   e. List of next of kin, with addresses, ages

   f. Will's date and names of witnesses to the will

   g. Original will

   h. Estimated total value of probate assets

   i. Request to waive bond if possible

   j. Filing fee for the court

2. *Appointment as personal representative.* Upon processing the initial filing, the court issues letters of authority, or the equivalent form, that authorizes you to proceed as the personal representative of the estate. If a bond is required, you will need to obtain and file this to finalize your appointment before receiving full authority to represent the estate. You should obtain several certified copies of your authorization to represent the estate as well because you will need it to show it to establish your right to deal with banks, creditors, debtors, government agencies, and others on behalf of the estate.

3. *Mail.* Arrange to obtain and continue to receive all decedent's mail. Do not pitch what appears to be "junk mail" without close examination.

4. *Next of kin.* The court will have forms for notifying next of kin (potential heirs by statute whether named in will or not). Also, locate and notify persons named as beneficiaries in the will that are not next of kin.

5. *Social Security Administration.* If this has not already been done by the funeral director or a family member, notify the SSA of the decedent's death, and determine if there is a death benefit available for surviving spouse or child of decedent. SSA can be reached at 800-772-1213 or at its local office. If the decedent was a veteran, similar notification should be made to the Veterans Administration. If the decedent has a surviving spouse, these agencies might require a copy of the marriage certificate and spouse's social security information as well as the death certificate and information about the decedent. Birth certificates for children might be required. They also might require a recent tax return. Also, survivor benefits might be available for a surviving spouse who is: age 60 or older; age 50 or older and disabled; or caring for children (disabled or minors) of the decedent.

6. *Estate bank account.* If the decedent left cash in the bank (or otherwise), open a bank checking account for the estate. You might be able to get one that pays interest. You will need your Letters of Authority (or equivalent) from the court for this. You can use decedent's bank or another bank that is convenient and preferable for you. Decedent's cash assets should be transferred to this account. If there are many cash assets, consider an investment account

to conserve and improve the estate's value as much as possible. This will be covered in more detail in Chapter 5, as will numbers 7 through 12 of this list.

7. *Inventory.* You need to review the decedent's papers and assets, as your first task is to prepare an inventory of all of the estate assets. You will need to contact institutions that hold decedent's accounts and investments to request up-to-date statements of accounts and value of them as of the date of death. Determine if assets need to be professionally appraised for value, if the decedent did not provide documentation of valuation applicable to time of death. Determine the location and value of assets, if any, that are itemized in the will; are any missing? List all other assets of the decedent. Items such as furniture can be listed as a group, unless specific pieces of exceptional value (e.g. antiques) need to be listed individually. Part of this process is identifying and opening decedent's safety deposit box(es).

8. *Life insurance.* Even if the estate is not a beneficiary of any life insurance, you will need to know the value and beneficiaries of life insurance if these amounts are includable in estate valuation for tax purposes in your state. If the estate is a beneficiary of life insurance, the proceeds come into the estate as a probate asset.

9. *Pension, profit sharing, annuities, deferred compensation.* Did decedent have any pension, profit sharing, annuities, or deferred compensation due from an employer? These might not be probate assets, depending on how they were set up, but they are includable in the estate value. Also, the estate could be a named beneficiary by the decedent, or the default beneficiary of other beneficiaries who

have predeceased the decedent. When the estate is the beneficiary, the proceeds are probate assets.

10. *Property insurance.* Make sure insurance coverage of probate property is transferred from the decedent's name to the estate. Most insurance companies will require a new policy issued to the estate. Contact the current insurance provider(s), and make sure all estate property is appropriately covered.

11. *Real property.* Determine the status of real property in which decedent had an interest and determine if it is probate property. Probate property is included on the Inventory. Non-probate property is included in the estate's tax valuation. Is any probate real estate out of state? If so, you will need to contact an attorney in that state to determine how transfer has to be done. Are real estate taxes owed?

12. *Professional assistance.* If you need appraisers for determining estate asset values, list the type of appraisers you need, and locate qualified people. Examples are: real estate, collectibles, artwork, vehicles, equipment, business entity, and livestock. You might decide you need a CPA to assist with tax returns or other accounting issues. You also might decide you need some legal assistance, whether to advise on handling the estate or for out-of-state property issues. Consult with your state's bar association if you do not know an attorney who specializes in estates and probate. Some states, like Ohio, have a certification process for attorneys that specialize in estates and trusts. You should seek out someone who has such certification, or, if such certification is not provided by your state, documented experience in this area of law.

13. *Creditor notice.* Determine the decedent's debts to the extent you can. Arrange for the publication of notice to creditors. This publication will notify any unknown creditors to make their claims timely or lose them. *This will be discussed in more detail in Chapter 6.*

14. *Trusts.* Are any trusts part of or relate to the estate? For example, did the decedent create a trust within the will? If so, there should be instructions within the will about this. Are existing independent trusts mentioned in the will's provisions? Are there trusts whose terms require disbursement of proceeds at death? Determine if such disbursement is part of the estate tax valuation. *This will be discussed in more detail in Chapter 7.*

15. *Surviving spouse/minor children.* Determine the needs for the surviving spouse and minor children. Are there any issues between them and the will's provisions? Does the spouse need to be notified of the right to "take against the will?" *Chapter 8 will give more information about this.*

16. *Tax returns.* Determine which taxes, if any, are applicable to the estate and the decedent. Make sure the tax returns are filed in a timely manner. *Taxes will be discussed in more detail in Chapter 9.*

17. *Estate business.* Once you have the inventory and debts in hand, you can assess whether the will can be carried out as the decedent wished. If is the estate has sufficient cash to satisfy all the estate costs and debts, the balance of the assets will be available for distribution. If any items named in the will are missing, you will need to determine what happened to them. Were they gifted to the beneficiary in advance? Did the decedent sell them or give them to

someone else? Is someone hiding them? Does property need to be liquidated for estate obligations? There might be court forms to file for this. *Many of these questions will be answered when you complete your Inventory Worksheet found in Chapter 5.*

18. *Closing the estate.* Final court filings are done to close the estate; court forms will guide you in this process. Once court costs and all other estate debts are paid, property can be distributed to beneficiaries. A final inventory is filed with the court and forms documenting distribution. It is a good practice to get a signed receipt from beneficiaries on disbursement. You need to document that you have satisfied the estate requirements. *This will be covered further in Chapter 10.*

Sample Probate Exercise

The following scenario is set up to walk you through a sample preparation of probate forms *(contained in the Appendix D and the CD-ROM of this book)* for probating a simple estate in the Lorain County Probate Court in the State of Ohio. The intent here is to familiarize you with using this form-driven process of probating a simple estate. Although states and courts differ from each other (and sometimes within the same court from case to case) in various details of procedure, more similarities than differences exist in the general process.

The Facts: Jason Little, a resident of Lorain County, Ohio, died of cancer on Sept. 25, 2011. You are Charlie Lightfoot, longtime friend of Jason. Jason was not married. He had been divorced some years ago and had no children. Jason had an advance health care directive in which he named you, with your consent, to be responsible for decisions if he could not be. However, Jason maintained ability to make his own decisions until his death.

Before he died, Jason told you that he had named you as his executor in his will, and he told you where the will was kept in his desk at his house. Jason also gave you a contract he had with the local funeral home, Heavenly Rest Memorial Chapel, that indicates he had prepaid the arrangements for his cremation. He instructed there be no service and that his ashes be given to you. Privately, Jason asked you to scatter his ashes on Lake Erie the next time you went fishing.

In late June 2011, Jason's condition reached the point where he maintained himself in bed at home, a rented house, with hospice care and a live-in nurse. In a hospice situation, no extraordinary life-saving measures are employed. The person is provided care and kept comfortable. Jason died peacefully the morning of September 25, 2011, at his home, with the hospice nurse and his private nurse both present. Heavenly Rest took care of the arrangements and notified you when the ashes were ready.

Emotions. Jason was a close friend. This is why you are in this situation and why you have agreed to the job of handling Jason's estate. This does not make it welcome or easy. Part of managing this work is dealing with your own emotions and grief. In this case, your friend has done some things to prepare you. You have been his designee on his advance health care directive; you and he discussed your being executor of his estate. You have been the one to make sure the funeral arrangements are carried out as he arranged for them. Nevertheless, do not be surprised to find these matters seem nearly overwhelming. It might feel like an invasion of Jason's privacy to be delving into his affairs. Keep in mind that Jason engaged you, with your consent, to do this for him. What do you do next?

The will and other matters

1. Check Jason's rented house, get the will, and secure his property. Under the circumstances of this situation, Jason already might have given you his will, but for whatever his reasons, he did not, and you respected his privacy. After his death, you immediately check the house, locate the will, and gather together papers and records. This should not be delayed. Make sure the house is secure. The live-in nurse might need a few days to arrange to leave, but more likely, she will want to move out quickly. Make sure the utilities remain in working order, mail and papers taken in, and trash set out on the proper day for pickup. Arrange with the landlord a date to remove Jason's property. Find out the status of the rent, how long it is paid up, and tenant obligations for cleaning on vacating the premises.

2. You have found Jason's will. Check the will to make sure: (a) it is the original showing Jason's signature, and (b) it is witnessed by the signatures of two witnesses. If it is not properly signed and witnessed, you will need to look for a completed original copy of the will in Jason's papers. If you cannot locate a completed will, Jason might not have finished his will properly, despite what he told you. If this turns out to be the case, then you would want to get advice of legal counsel at this point. If there is no legally executed will, then Jason died intestate. The estate will be processed and assets disbursed according to state law. Although you might still be the best person to manage the estate, you will want guidance on the legal implications under intestate procedure. Because you are not a blood relative, you would not be entitled to anything from his

estate, other than fees as the administrator if you were appointed. In this case, you find Jason's will in his desk, right where he said it would be, and it appears to be in order as the original will with Jason's signature and the signatures of two witnesses.

Last Will and Testament of Jason Little

I, Jason Little, being of sound mind and knowing the measure of all I possess, declare this document to be my last will and testament made on July 10th in the year 2011. I revoke all prior wills and codicils.

1. I name as my Executor, Charles Lightfoot, who shall serve without bond. In the event he cannot, or declines, to serve as Executor, then I name Thrifty Bank of Elyria, Ohio, to serve as Executor.

2. I direct my Executor to make sure my funeral arrangements are handled according to the prepaid instructions and arrangements I have made with Heavenly Rest Memorial Chapel of Lorain, Ohio; to pay the taxes and all debts, if any such be due, of my estate; to disburse the specific bequests and residue of my estate as I have directed herein; and to undertake all other such business as may be necessary to settle the affairs of my estate. My Executor is to be reimbursed from the estate for any and all costs he may incur in administering the estate in addition to his lawful executor's administration fees as approved by the Court.

3. Specific Bequests I: I leave to my good friend Charles Lightfoot, the following items:
   (a) all my fishing gear; and
   (b) the sum of $10,000.

4. Specific Bequests II: I leave to my nurse, Thelma Goodbody, who has cared for me during my illness, the sum of $5,000; and

5. Specific Bequests III: I leave to the Scholarship Fund of The Perch Club of Lorain, Ohio, $1,000; and

6. The rest, residue, and balance of my estate, should there be any such remaining after such bequests are satisfied and debts and obligations are paid, I leave to my good friend Charles Lightfoot. If Charles Lightfoot predeceases me, then the residue shall pass to the Lake Erie Fish and Game Preservation Club of Lorain County, Ohio.

7. Any person who makes a claim to my estate against this will (whether such person is named herein or not) in contravention of my wishes shall be forthwith disinherited and disavowed of any and all such claim and any and all bequests made to him or her in this will. It is my express intent and direction that any person who chooses to fight against my wishes and divert any of my property otherwise than as directed herein, shall not benefit from such dispute, from my estate or from this will.

Signed of my own free knowledge without any restraint upon me on this 10th day of July 2011, this, my Last Will and Testament, at 2 Pike Place, Lorain, Ohio 44052.

Jason Little

Signed in the Presence of:

WCWcConnell, who resides at 403n TR Lane, Lorain, OH 44053

Betsy Dicken, who resides at 94 Loose Stone Rd., Kipton, OH

3. Obtain the Probate Court forms. Jason was a resident of Lorain County, so you need the forms and procedure for filing a will with the Lorain County Probate Court. This court has its forms online, which makes your job easier.

File the will and apply to be appointed executor

This is a simple will. There are three beneficiaries: Thelma Good-body, you (Charles Lightfoot), and The Perch Club of Lorain Scholarship Fund. The will is the original, signed, and witnessed.

So that you have the authority to round up Jason's property, bank accounts, handle his debts and bequests, and other matters of the estate, you need to be appointed as his estate's executor by the Lorain County Probate Court.

To file application to probate the will with the court and apply to be appointed executor, you need to complete the necessary probate court forms. *The relevant Lorain County Probate forms are included in the Appendix D of this book.* Note that along with the will, you (Charlie) need to file a certified death certificate, which proves the death of the testator (Jason Little) and date of death (September 25, 2011).

These are illustrative examples of key forms required to process the hypothetical estate of Jason Little according to the information provided on the website of the Lorain County Probate Court, Ohio. There also might be a filing of the notice of publication of the estate in the newspaper and possibly other filings required by the court, depending on the circumstances of a real estate. Having a good grasp of the court forms, though, is more than half the battle of processing the court procedure for administering a simple estate.

Probate forms

Attach the will and death certificate to Probate Court Form 2.0 Application to Probate the Will. File Form 1.0 with it. As named beneficiaries in the will, The Perch Club and Thelma Goodbody have a right to notice of probate. You contact them before filing, give them a copy of the will, and ask them to sign the waiver on the first page of Form 2.0. At the same time, you ask them to sign Form 4.0 on page 2 for Waiver of Notice of your Application for Authority to Administer the Estate. They agree and sign both of them. Getting these waivers is not essential to probating the will or becoming appointed, but it speeds up the process. With the waivers, the court must set a hearing date and time. If the hearing date and time passes without anyone contesting the applications, then the court can proceed to approve the applications.

Prepare a check payable to the court for the filing fee. You will be reimbursed from the estate for this cost.

File the form to probate the will with the original will and the death certificate with the Probate Court by taking the documents and filing fee to the Clerk of Courts for the Probate Court in the county courthouse.

When the court approves the will, file Probate Form 4.0. Application for Authority to Administer Estate, Form 4.3 Waiver of Right to Administer and Form 1.0. These forms are necessary for you to be appointed as executor for Jason's estate.

LORAIN COUNTY PROBATE COURT
JUDGE JAMES T. WALTHER

ESTATE OF _____, DECEASED

CASE NO. _____

APPLICATION TO PROBATE WILL
[R.C. 2107.11, 2107.18, and 2107.19]

Applicant states that decedent died on _____

Decedent's domicile was _____
Street Address

City or Village, or Township if unincorporated area   County

Post Office   State   Zip Code

A document purporting to be decedent's last will is attached and offered for probate, and applicant waives notice of probate of this will.

Decedent's surviving spouse, children, next of kin, and legatees and devisees, known to applicant, are listed on the attached Form 1.0.

Attorney for Applicant   Applicant

Typed or Printed Name   Typed or Printed Name

Address   Address

Phone Number (include area code)   Phone Number (include area code)

Attorney Registration No. _____

WAIVER OF NOTICE OF PROBATE OF WILL

The undersigned, being persons entitled to notice of the probate of this will, waive such notice. After a certificate is filed evidencing these waivers and any notices given, any action to contest the validity of this will must be filed no more than three months after the filing of the certificate for estates of decedents who die on or after January 1, 2002, and no more than four months after the filing of the certificate for estates of decedents who die before January 1, 2002.

FORM 2.0 - APPLICATION TO PROBATE WILL   12/01/2002

CASE NO. _____

ENTRY ADMITTING WILL TO PROBATE

The Court finds that the purported will of decedent, either on its face or from testimony of the witnesses, complies with applicable law. It is therefore admitted to probate and ordered recorded. The Court further orders that notice of the probate be given to all parties entitled to notice.

_____   _____
               Date   Judge

CERTIFICATE OF WAIVER OF NOTICE

The undersigned states that all persons entitled to notice:

[Check applicable boxes]

☐ Have waived notice of the application for probate of this will or of a contest as to jurisdiction.

☐ Have waived notice of this will's admission to probate. The waivers are filed herein.

☐ Have not been notified because their names or places of residence are unknown and cannot with reasonable diligence be ascertained.

_____
☐ Fiduciary
☐ Applicant for the admission of this will to probate
☐ Applicant for a release from administration
☐ Other interested person
☐ Attorney for any of the above

Attorney Registration No. _____

FORM 2.0 - APPLICATION TO PROBATE WILL   12/01/2002

LORAIN COUNTY PROBATE COURT
JUDGE JAMES T. WALTHER

ESTATE OF _____, DECEASED

CASE NO. _____

APPLICATION FOR AUTHORITY TO ADMINISTER ESTATE

[R.C. 2109.02 and 2109.07]

[For Executors and all Administrators; attach supplemental
application for ancillary administration, if applicable]

Applicant states that decedent died on _____

Decedent's domicile was _____

Street Address

City or Village, or Township if unincorporated Area   County

Post Office   State   Zip Code

Applicant asks to be appointed _____

of decedent's estate. [Check whichever of the following are applicable] - ☐ To applicant's knowledge, decedent did not leave a will - ☐ Decedent's Will has been admitted to probate in this Court - ☐ A supplemental application for ancillary administration is attached.

Attached is a list of the surviving spouse, children, next of kin, and legatees and devisees, known to applicant, which list includes those persons entitled to administer the estate.

The estimated value of the estate is:

Personal property.. $ _____

Subtotal, personality and rentals.. $ _____

Real Property... $ _____

Total estimated estate... $ _____

Applicant owes the estate.. $ _____

The estate owes applicant... $ _____

[Check one of the following four paragraphs]

☐ Applicant says that decedent's Will requests that no bond be required, and therefore asks the Court to dispense with bond.

☐ Applicant is a trust company duly qualified in Ohio, and bond is dispensed with by law.

FORM 4.0 - APPLICATION FOR AUTHORITY TO ADMINISTER ESTATE

CASE NO. _____

☐ Applicant is decedent's surviving spouse, and is entitled to the entire net proceeds of the estate or is in the next of kin Entitled to the entire net proceeds of the estate and there is no will, therefore bond dispensed with by law.

☐ Applicant offers the attached bond in the amount of $ _____.

Applicant accepts the duties of fiduciary in the estate imposed by law and such additional duties as may be required by the Court. Applicant acknowledges being subject to removal as fiduciary for failure to perform such duties as required and also acknowledges being subject to criminal penalties for improper conversion of any property help as fiduciary.

_____   _____
Attorney for Applicant   **Applicant**

_____   _____
Typed or Printed Name   **Typed or Printed Name**

_____   _____
Address   **Address**

_____   _____

_____   _____
Phone Number (include area code)   **Phone Number (include area code)**
Attorney Registration No. _____

WAIVER OF RIGHT TO ADMINISTER
[R.C. 2109.02 and 2109.07]

The undersigned, being persons entitled to administer decedent's estate, and whose priority of right to do so is equal or superior to that of applicant, hereby waive appointment to administer the estate.

_____   _____
_____   _____
_____   _____
_____   _____

ENTRY SETTING HEARING AND ORDERING NOTICE

The Court sets_____, at _____o'clock_____ M. as the date and time for hearing the application for authority to administer decedent's estate. The Court orders notice to take or renounce administration to be given those persons entitled to administer decedent's estate, whose priority of right to do so is equal or superior to that of applicant and who have not waived appointment to administer the estate.

_____   _____
Date   **Probate Judge**

FORM 4.0 - APPLICATION FOR AUTHORITY TO ADMINISTER ESTATE

Lorain CountyProbate Court
Judge James T. Walther

ESTATE OF _____, DECEASED

CASE NO. _____

SURVIVING SPOUSE, CHILDREN, NEXT OF KIN,
LEGATEES AND DEVISEES
[R.C. 2105.06, 2106.13 and 2107.19]

**[Use with those applications or filings requiring some or all of the
information in this form, for notice or other purposes. Update as required.]**

The following are decedent's known surviving spouse, children, and the lineal descendants of deceased children. If none, the following are decedent's next of kin who are or would be entitled to inherit under the statutes of descent and distribution.

Name	Residence Address	Relationship to Decedent	Birthdate of Minor
		Surviving Spouse	

[Check whichever of the following is applicable]

☐   The surviving spouse is the natural or adoptive parent of all of the decedent's children.

☐   The surviving spouse is the natural or adoptive parent of at least one, but not all, of the decedent's children.

☐   The surviving spouse is not the natural or adoptive parent of any of the decedent's children.

☐   There are minor children of the decedent who are not the children of the surviving spouse.

☐   There are minor children of the decedent and no surviving spouse.

FORM 1.0 - SURVIVING SPOUSE, CHILDREN, NEXT OF KIN, LEGATEES AND DEVISEES   12/01/2002

CASE NO. _____

The following are the vested beneficiaries named in the decedent's will:

Name	Residence Address	Birthdate of minor

[Check whichever of the following is applicable]

☐ The will contains a charitable trust or a bequest or devise to a charitable trust, subject to R.C. 109.23 to 109.41.

☐ The will is not subject to R.C. 109.23 to 109.41 relating to charitable trusts.

_____   _____
Date   Applicant (or give other title)

_____

FORM 1.0 - SURVIVING SPOUSE, CHILDREN, NEXT OF KIN, LEGATEES AND DEVISEES   12/01/2002

Upon appointment as executor

Upon review of the application you have filed, and there being no objections to due to the waivers you obtained, the court issues an order appointing you as executor of Jason's estate. Now you obtain a Federal Employer Tax ID number for the estate of Jason Little from the IRS. This can be done online at **www.irs.gov**. This ID number will be needed to open an estate bank account and for any tax filings that might be necessary for the estate.

Open an estate checking account with the bank of your choice. The bank will need the Federal Employer Tax ID number, a copy of the order appointing you as executor from the court, and probably a copy of the death certificate. You decide to use Thrifty, Jason's bank, for convenience. You open the estate account and close Jason's accounts with the money in them transferred to the estate account.

Determine the value of the estate assets

When you filed your application to be appointed executor, you had a good idea of the estate's value because you had access to Jason's papers, including his bank books. You knew what he had in the bank and what he had in the way of physical (tangible) property. Due to his last illness, Jason had sold his truck and boat several months before he died, something you already knew. Thus, there are no vehicles in the estate. His house was rented. His property consists of his personal property of clothing, furniture, the fishing equipment, and the money from his bank accounts. You had estimated the estate at $62,000 — the $60,000 in the bank plus $2,000 as a round number for the fishing gear and miscellaneous personal possessions until the latter can be assessed more precisely.

The court has a list of approved appraisers, but you do not find any that qualify for fishing gear. You ask a local fishing guide, who is also a fishing gear retailer, if he could appraise Jason's fishing gear; he agrees. He values the fishing gear at $1,000 (slightly lower than you thought it might be). You have him sign the appraiser certificate on page 1 of Probate Court Form 6.0 Inventory and Appraisal. You also have Thelma Goodbody and The Perch Club Secretary sign waiver of hearing on the inventory, also on Form 6.0. You value the miscellaneous household goods at $500. Jason did not own anything of value. His furniture is old, as are his clothes. Jason took care of his belongings, but his needs were simple and focused on fishing. Even his TV set was old. He preferred his fishing guides and his old shortwave radio.

You determine that the miscellaneous personal household effects, furniture, and clothes, as Jason's only other physical property, can be listed at a nominal value of $500. These items can be estimated, as they are not of special value.

Jason did not have stocks and bonds, but he had the two bank accounts; one is a money market account with $50,000 and the other is a checking account with $10,000. They are in Thrifty Bank, the same bank as the estate bank account you opened. You arranged with the bank for these accounts to be closed and the funds to be moved into the estate's bank account. You have found no evidence that Jason had a safety deposit box anywhere — no key, no documentation — and Thrifty confirms this.

You file Form 6.0, Inventory and Appraisal along with a copy of Form 1.0 with the Court.

LORAIN COUNTY PROBATE COURT
JUDGE JAMES T. WALTHER

ESTATE OF _____ , DECEASED

CASE NO. _____

INVENTORY AND APPRAISAL
[R.C. 2115.02 and 2115.09]

To the knowledge of the fiduciary the attached schedule of assets in decedent's estate is complete. The fiduciary determined the value of those assets whose values were readily ascertainable and which were not appraised by the appraiser, and that such values are correct.

The estate is recapitulated as follows:

Tangible personal property..$_____

Intangible personal property..$_____

Real property..$_____

Total..$_____

First automobile transferred to surviving spouse under R.C. 2106.18   value $_____
Second automobile transferred to surviving spouse under R.C. 2106.18   value $_____

Total value [not to exceed $40,000.00].. $ _____

Insofar as it can be ascertained, an Ohio Estate Tax Return ☐will ☐ will not be filed.

☐ The fiduciary is also the surviving spouse of the decedent and waives notice of the taking of the inventory.

_____   _____
Attorney   Fiduciary

Attorney Registration No. _____

APPRAISER'S CERTIFICATE

The undersigned appraiser agrees to act as appraiser of decedent's estate and to appraise the property exhibited truly, honestly, impartially, and to the best of the appraiser's knowledge and ability. The appraiser further says that those assets whose values were not readily ascertainable are indicated on the attached schedule by a check in the "Appraised" column opposite each such item, and that such values are correct.

_____
Appraiser

FORM 6.0 - INVENTORY AND APPRAISAL   12/01/2002

(Reverse of Form 6.0)

CASE NO. _____

WAIVER OF NOTICE OF TAKING OF INVENTORY
[R.C. 2115.04]

The undersigned surviving spouse hereby waives notice of the time and place of taking the inventory of decedent's estate.

_____

Surviving Spouse

WAIVER OF NOTICE OF HEARING ON INVENTORY
[Use when notice is required by the Court or deemed necessary by the fiduciary]

The undersigned, who are interested in the estate, waive notice of the hearing on the inventory.

_____   _____

_____   _____

_____   _____

_____   _____

_____   _____

_____   _____

_____   _____

ENTRY SETTING HEARING

The Court sets _____ at _____ o'clock _____.M., as the date and time for hearing the inventory of decedent's estate.

_____   _____
Date   Judge

Chapter 3: Probate Procedure

LORAIN COUNTY PROBATE COURT
JUDGE JAMES T. WALTHER

ESTATE OF _____, DECEASED

CASE NO. _____

SCHEDULE OF ASSETS

(Attach to inventory and appraisal)

Page _____ of _____ pages.

(Insert a check in the column "Appraised" opposite an item if it was valued by the appraiser. Leave blank if the readily ascertainable value was determined by fiduciary)

Item	Appraised	Value
		$

FORM 6.1 - SCHEDULE OF ASSETS   10/1/98

(Reverse of Form 6.1)

Page _____ of _____ pages.

Item	Appraised	Value
		$

Fiduciary

Give notice to creditors

First, you put a public notice in the newspaper. You prepare and arrange for publication of the notice to creditors according to the court's requirements.

Then, you send out a direct letter to all known creditors. Based on the mail that has come in for Jason, you are aware of specific creditors, most of them relating to Jason's final illness. You send them the following letter:

Your Letterhead

Date

Creditor Name and Address

Re: Estate of Jason Little

Dear (Creditor Name):

I am the Executor of the Estate of Jason Little, No. X123 in the Lorain County Probate Court. As you may be aware, Mr. Little died on September 25, 2011. If you have a claim of account receivable for services rendered to Mr. Little, please forward to me at the address shown above, an itemized statement describing the services, name(s) of person(s) providing the services and dates the services were provided. I am not able to evaluate and resolve any claim you may have until I receive complete information.

Thank you for your attention to this matter.

Very truly yours,

/S/

Charles Lightfoot

For Ohio estates, creditors have up to six months from the date of death to file their claims with the estate. After that, they are foreclosed. Therefore, it is prudent to wait the six months before closing out the estate to be sure all creditor claims are captured and foreclosed. In the meantime, you pay the known debts.

According to the responses you have received from creditor notices you have mailed and published in the newspaper, you find that the debts to be paid for Jason are:

Debts re:	Jason's final illness:		$12,000
	Philip Waters, M.D.	$2,000	
	Lord Have Mercy Hospital	$3,500	
	Fortune Health Services	$2,000	
	Blue Cloud Hospice	$2,000	
	Home Med EquiSupplies	$1,500	
	Airwing SoftTransport	$1,000	
	Jason's landlord (final rent):		$ 200
	Private Nurse (final):		$1,000
	Final utilities/rental house:		$ 150
	Great Lakes Fish and Gear (appraiser)		$ 20

You pay the known debts and the estate appraiser. You reimburse yourself for the court costs and any other expenses you have incurred on behalf of the estate.

Considering that you are the residuary beneficiary as well as the beneficiary of a special bequest of $10,000 and the fishing gear, you decide you will waive your fees. Nevertheless, because you are the estate fiduciary as well as a beneficiary, you make sure you keep track of your time handling the estate business. You carefully keep your time sheet of the estate work you perform so you will be able to show that you executed your duties appropriately. If you change your mind and decide you should apply for fees, you will have the time sheets to support them.

Taking care of the taxes

The estate is not large enough to require federal estate tax filing ($5.12 million exemption for 2012). Also, the estate is under the $385,000 for Ohio estate tax liability to be triggered. Because of his illness, Jason did not earn income in 2012 in a large enough amount to require a federal form 1040 or equivalent personal income tax filing.

Closing the estate — Final probate forms filed

For purposes of this hypothetical case study, you (Charlie Lightfoot) have prepared Probate Court 13 as the Final Account to close the estate. In a real circumstance, you would include the date you have prepared the form for filing. When the estate is filed, the court rules or the judge's orders, depending on the court, will provide you with action dates, including the filing of forms such as the Final Account. If the estate's business is not complete, you can file a Partial Account, which advises the status of the work on the estate to date. In this case, it is the same Form 13, with the box checked for "partial" instead of "final" account.

Lorain County Probate Court Judge James T. Walther

ESTATE OF _____, DECEASED

CASE NO. _____

FIDUCIARY'S ACCOUNT
[R.C. 2109.30, 2109.301 and 2109.32]

[Executors and Administrators]

The fiduciary offers the account given below and on the attached itemized statement of receipts and disbursements. The fiduciary states that the account is correct, and asks that it be approved and settled.

[Check one of the following]

☐ This is a partial account. A statement of the assets remaining in the fiduciary's hands is attached.

☐ This is a final account. A statement of the assets remaining in the fiduciary's hands for distribution to the beneficiaries is attached.

☐ This is an account of distribution, and fiduciary asks to be discharged upon its approval and settlement.

☐ This is a final and distributive account, and the fiduciary asks to be discharged upon its approval and settlement.

☐ This is a supplemental final account.

[Complete if this is a partial account, or if one or more accounts have previously been filed in the estate] The period of this account is from _____ to _____

[Complete if applicable] Accounts previously filed in the estate, the accounting periods, and the fiduciary and attorney fees paid for each period, are as follows:

Date Filed	Accounting Period	Fiduciary Fees Paid	Attorney Fees Paid
		$	$

Note:
2117.06(K) states: "The distributee may be liable to the estate up to the value of the distribution and may be required to return all or any part of the value of the distribution if a valid claim is subsequently made against the estate within the time permitted under this section."
2109.32(C) states: "The rights of any person with a pecuniary interest in the estate are not barred by approval of an account pursuant to division (A) and (B) of this section. These rights may be barred following a hearing on the account pursuant to section 2109.33 of the Revised Code."

13.0 - FIDUCIARY'S ACCOUNT   12/01/2002

Case No. _____

This account is recapitulated as follows:

RECEIPTS

Personal property not sold . . . . $_____

Proceeds from sale of personal property. . . . . _____

Real property not sold. . . . . _____

Proceeds from sale of real property. . . . . _____

Income. . . . . _____

Other receipts. . . . . _____

Total receipts . . . . $_____

DISBURSEMENTS

Fiduciary fees this accounting period . . . . $_____

Attorney fees this accounting period . . . .   _____

Other administration costs and expenses. . . . .   _____

Debts and claims against estate . . . .   _____

Ohio and federal estate taxes . . . .   _____

Personal property distributed in kind . . . .   _____

Real property transferred . . . .   _____

Other distributions to beneficiaries . . . .   _____

Other disbursements . . . .   _____

Total disbursements . . . . $_____

BALANCE REMAINING IN FIDUCIARY'S HANDS . . . . $_____

_____   _____
Attorney   Fiduciary

Attorney Registration No. _____   Date_____

ENTRY SETTING HEARING

The Court sets _____ at _____ o'clock _____ M., as the date and time for hearing the
above account.

Date_____ Judge_____

Lorain County Probate Court
Judge James T. Walther

ESTATE OF _____, DECEASED

CASE NO. _____

RECEIPTS AND DISBURSEMENTS

[Attach to fiduciary's account]

Page _____ of _____ pages

Following is an itemized statement of receipts and disbursements by the fiduciary in the administration of his trust.

Item	Voucher No.	Value or Amount
		$

13.1 - RECEIPTS AND DISBURSEMENTS

Page _____ of _____ pages

Item	Voucher No.	Value or Amount
		$

Fiduciary

Lorain County Probate Court
Judge James T. Walther

ESTATE OF _____, **DECEASED**

CASE NO. _____

WAIVER OF PARTIAL ACCOUNT
[R.C. 2109.30(B)(2)]

Partial Account due _____

The fiduciary says that all of the decedent's legatees, devisees, or heirs have waived the above partial account. This waiver is accordingly presented in lieu of the partial account.

_____   _____
Date   Fiduciary

The undersigned legatees, devisees, or heirs of decedent not under legal disability hereby waive the filing of the above partial account by the fiduciary, and consent to the filing of this waiver in lieu thereof.

Legatees, Devisees, or Heirs:

_____   _____

_____   _____

_____   _____

_____   _____

_____   _____

_____   _____

_____   _____

_____   _____

_____   _____

_____   _____

FORM 13.4 - WAIVER OF PARTIAL ACCOUNT   3/1/96

Lorain County Probate Court
Judge James T. Walther

ESTATE OF _____, DECEASED

CASE NO. _____

CERTIFICATE OF TERMINATION
[R.C. 2109.30]

I certify I am the executor or administrator and the sole legatee, devisee or heir.

I further certify:

    (1)   all debts and claims presented to the estate have been paid in full or settled finally;

    (2)   an estate tax return, if required under Chapter 5731 of the Revised Code, has been filed, and any estate tax due under that chapter has been paid;

    (3)   all attorney fees have been [check one] ☐ waived by counsel of record, ☐ paid to counsel of record in the amount of $ _____;

    (4)   all fiduciary fees have been [check one] ☐ waived by the fiduciary; ☐ paid to the fiduciary in the amount of $ _____;

    (5)   all assets remaining after completion of the activities described above have been distributed to myself as the sole legatee, devisee or heir.

_____   _____
Attorney for Fiduciary   Fiduciary

Attorney Registration No. _____

ENTRY

Based upon the above certification it is ordered that the fiduciary and surety, if any, are discharged.

_____
Judge

FORM 13.6 - CERTIFICATE OF TERMINATION   3/1/96

Lorain County Probate Court
Judge James T. Walther

ESTATE OF _____, DECEASED

CASE NO. _____

WAIVER OF NOTICE OF HEARING ON ACCOUNT
[R.C. 2109.33]

The undersigned, who are interested in the estate, waive notice of the hearing on the account.

_____   _____

_____   _____

_____   _____

_____   _____

_____   _____

_____   _____

_____   _____

_____   _____

_____   _____

_____   _____

_____   _____

_____   _____

FORM 13.7 - WAIVER OF NOTICE OF HEARING ON ACCOUNT   3/1/96

Lorain County Probate Court
Judge James T. Walther

ESTATE OF _____

CASE NO. _____

CERTIFICATE OF SERVICE OF ACCOUNT
TO HEIRS OR BENEFICIARIES
[R.C. 2109.32]

This is to certify that a true and accurate copy of the _____ account was

Type of Account

served _____ upon all beneficiaries of the estate except:

Date

☐   The following heir or beneficiary whose address is unknown: _____

_____

☐   The following beneficiary of a specific bequest or devise who has received his or her distribution
and for which a receipt has been filed or exhibited with the Court:

_____

_____   _____
Attorney   Fiduciary

Attorney Registration No._____

Note that the itemized listing includes a "voucher" number. This is the number of the check from the estate checking account that you wrote to pay the bill. The invoice copy and/or paid receipt should be kept in your with a copy of the check. This is the "backup" documentation of the estate's debts and expenses. Most courts do not require the actual check copies and receipts to be filed with the Final Account these days, but some may. You have to find out what the court requires in this regard.

One receipt that will have to filed is the paid funeral expense. In the case of Jason's prepaid funeral bill, you as Charlie Lightfoot would label the prepaid funeral bill as "No. 1" with the paid receipt and attach it to show the funeral bill was paid by Jason pre-death. The Court will review the Final Fiduciary's Account and supporting documentation and either approve it to close the estate, have a hearing to review questions, or return it to you for revision and resubmittal. The latter can occur if the court finds a technical problem with the way the form has been completed, requests additional documentation for a particular debt, or finds an error on the form or in the documentation. Also, if Charlie had not had waivers from Thelma Goodbody and The Perch Club on the Final Fiduciary Account, the court likely would have set a hearing to be sure their rights were covered before closing the estate.

In the Estate of Jason Little, we will consider the case closed at this point. You have covered all the procedural, paperwork bases with Charlie Lightfoot for this hypothetical simple estate.

Having shadowed Charlie Lightfoot through these action items of the Estate of Jason Little, you should have a sense of the forms and steps in the personal representative's obligations for the estate. The keys to success are keeping track of the details, paying attention to the court rules, completing all the necessary forms and being methodical in working through the required tasks in a logical, efficient sequence, and then filing the required forms timely with the probate court.

Jason made your and Charlie's job easy. He took care of things in a straightforward way before he died. He wrote a simple and clearly stated will. He discussed appointment of Charlie as his executor with Charlie beforehand, told Charlie where to find the will, and gave him the key to his house. Jason might have made the process even easier by making gifts of his special bequests, or at the least, the noncash item (fishing gear) to Charlie, before he died. This would have removed the fishing gear from probate, and Charlie would not have had to go through the process of getting the gear appraised and authority for transfer to himself "in kind."

That Jason chose not do this illustrates that people are not always ready to part with their possessions, even when it seems to be the reasonable option. It might not be so much about the possessions themselves as what they represent to the testator. In Jason's case, it is clear that fishing was an important part of his life. He methodically put much of his life in order as he faced his terminal illness. He sold his car and even his boat, but he was not ready to part with his fishing gear. Perhaps he held on to the hope that he would have one more chance to go fishing with his friend. While he still had his gear, the hope was real. Jason did do the right thing about the few possessions he had, though. He made sure his money, his fishing gear, and anything else left over would be dispersed as he wanted it to be, by writing his will. He did not leave it to his friend Charlie to take care of his affairs for him without having any authority to do so.

CASE STUDY:
TIPS FROM A JUDGE

Judge Weldon Copeland
Probate Court One
Collin County Court at Law
University Drive Courts Facility
McKinney, TX

Note: These answers are generalizations and simplifications of complex legal issues. Every situation is unique, and you should consult your own lawyer before making any legal decisions.

There are many different sides to the probate story, and it is often helpful to look at the probate process from several different angles. Judge Weldon Copeland provided a look at the probate process from the opposite side of the courtroom, long after the drafting of the will and the planning of the estate has ceased. Even though Judge Copeland handles the complexities of probate every day, he was quick to note that he has nothing to do with the process of planning it while presiding in probate court.

"Probate judges do little or nothing in the will planning and estate-planning process," he began. "Occasionally, a probate judge will be asked to construe or modify the terms of a trust that was created in the estate-planning process, but probate judges are not often otherwise called upon to take action in an estate-planning matter. A substantial purpose of estate planning is undertaken to avoid — or at least minimize — probate court proceedings. Still, even good estate planning sometimes will leave a need for some minimal action in the probate court after a death."

Judge Copeland did note that it is very important to have a will, trust, and designated power of attorney.

"The importance of having a will is determined by the circumstances and the intentions/desires of the individual involved," he said. "First and obviously, some people will want to pass their probate estate to one or more persons who would not inherit in the absence of a will under the descent and distribution/intestacy statutes. To pass an estate to another who would not inherit as an intestate heir, there needs to be a will or actions taken to place the deceased's assets into joint tenancies or trusts that will avoid the need to probate the estate. But even those who want to pass their estate to the people who would inherit under the descent and distribution/intestacy statutes often will desire to have the additional benefits that a will can provide."

Judge Copeland said that individuals can add provisions to a will that will streamline the administration of the estate and simplify many aspects of the probate process. For example, a person can name the individual who will administer the estate in the will and instruct that this person not be required to post bond. Without this designation in the will, a court may require that the executor post a bond to ensure that he or she carries out his or her duties to administer the estate in good faith. The bond helps to ensure that the executor does not commit fraud against the estate or embezzle any amounts from the estate. By designating the executor in the will and instructing that no bond needs to be posted, the testator removes a possible burden from the court and the shoulders of the executor. Similarly, individuals also may designate in their will the person they wish to serve as the guardian of their children if both parents should die. This will eliminate the need for the court to appoint a guardian in such a situation.

"People with extremely large estates can achieve substantial tax advantages through trusts created in a will," Judge Copeland explained. "Because the existence of a will can preclude access to the simplified small estate procedures under the Texas Probate Code, people with small estates that will not require administration, those estates worth less than $50,000, plus exempt property of any value, might be better off without a will. However, even those with small estates need a will if they wish to pass their probate estate differently than the intestacy laws."

Chapter 4

Wills

*a*s mentioned in the previous chapter, your first step in the probate process is to read the will. This chapter will help you understand the legalities and purpose of a will and the pertinent information it contains.

Wills Defined

A person's last will and testament is a legal document that sets forth the person's — the testator's — directions for distribution of his or her property. Other considerations might be covered, such as guardianship of minors and care for pets. To be legal, a will must include a number of elements. The will needs to identify the date, the testator's full name, the names of beneficiaries, an executor or executrix, and the directions the testator intends to be carried out for his or her property and loved ones.

The basic will elements thus include:

- **Beneficiary:** The individual(s) or group(s) who will receive the testator's property. There will be at least one.

- **Executor/Executrix:** The will identifies the estate's personal representative, the individual who will handle the testator's probate property. If there is no will, the court appoints an administrator, usually the testator's spouse or adult child, who will serve in the same capacity of handling all the paperwork, preparing of assets, dealing with likely heirs, handling claims from creditors, making payments of outstanding debts, and other estate-related matters.

- **Clauses:** The sections of the will that organize the information in a specific order.

    o **Opening clauses:** Identify the testator and set the stage for the clauses that follow:

    - Introductory clause identifies the person who is making the will and generally states the testator is of sound mind and intends this to be his or her will.

    - Family statement clause introduces and identifies the family members who will be referred to later in the will.

    - Tax/debts clause explains how the taxes and debts of the estate will be paid. This clause sometimes is found toward the end of the will or with the Executor clause.

    o **Guardianship clause:** The appointment of a guardian for minor children (under the age of 18); a successor guardian also should be named as a backup.

o **Giving clauses:** These clauses are the specific bequests of property that are each identified by name and description to beneficiaries and explain what property goes to which person and under what circumstances, usually according to the following categories:

- **Real property clauses:** Statements that match up property with a person. For example: the family home to a spouse, a summer home to a son, a rental duplex to named children equally

- **Personal property clauses:** Used for explicit bequests of items. For example: Google® stock to brother Fred, Rolex® to nephew Tim, grand piano to daughter Phoebe

o **Residuary clause, or residue:** This accounts for the "leftovers," the balance of the estate that is not itemized in a list. It is a catch all that ensures all other property is accounted for in the will. The residuary clause is essential for any kind of will to make sure that anything the testator might have overlooked or acquired after writing the will can be distributed lawfully. Otherwise, there is a risk that part of the probate estate will be intestate because it is outside the will. Naming at least one residuary beneficiary is an essential will provision for this reason.

o **Appointment clause:** Identifies the personal representative, who will manage the estate.

o **Fiduciary powers clause:** The language that gives the personal representative the power to serve as your executor, including any duties that go beyond the basic requirements established by law. For example: " James

Allen, my Executor, shall have the power to provide for my spouse and children out of the assets of my asset until the estate is settled." Another power usually spelled out is the personal representative's power to sell estate assets to pay debts and provide for spouse and/or minor children.

o **Ending clauses:** These include the legalities to meet statutory requirements so that the will is legal and valid, which include (but are not limited to) the testator's signature, date, location of the signing, and witnesses.

Once a will is filed in probate court, it becomes public information, which means that anyone can read it. Knowing this, some people write their wills rather broadly and leave it to their executors to manage the details outside the public eye as much as possible. This puts a burden on the personal representative in determining the intent of the testator when a beneficiary disagrees.

Will Basics

Essentials elements for a valid will include:

- **A writing.** Oral wills are recognized in rare and limited circumstances and in only few states because proving them is difficult. No oral declaration will be able to dispose of a person's estate fully.

- **Testator's name and age.** The testator must be of lawful age to make a will for the state of residence. For most states, this is age 18.

- **"Being of sound mind."** This means the testator was mentally competent to know and understand the property in his or her possession at the time of making the will, as well as the persons (whether people or institutions) identified as beneficiaries.

- **Clear statement of intention to transfer property.** This is satisfied by a clear statement that the testator intends the document to be his or will and that the purpose therefore is the final wishes to disperse property.

- **Signed voluntarily.** A will that is coerced in whole or in part is not valid.

- **Witnessed properly.** Two competent adults are all that is needed, but state law always should be checked to be sure the witnesses are proper and the signing properly done. For example, many, but not all, states allow a witness also to be a beneficiary of the will. Even if state law permits it though, it is not a good practice because it raises a question of coercion or at least a conflict of interest. If a beneficiary is also a witness, be aware that there is a potential issue of validity.

- **Executed properly.** The will must include a statement that attests to the fact that the document is indeed the testator's will; it must state the date and the place it is signed; and that it is signed in front of the witnesses who have signed it.

CASE STUDY:
TIPS FROM AN ATTORNEY

Donald Ray Burger, attorney at law
Houston, Texas
www.burger.com

Donald Ray Burger has been an attorney and worked with wills and probate for more than 19 years. Burger was admitted to the practice of law in Texas in 1979. In addition to being licensed in Texas, he is licensed to practice in the southern, eastern, and western Federal District Courts of Texas and the U.S. Fifth Circuit Court of Appeals.

Although Burger does believe it is important to have a will, he also points out that most people probably do not need a trust. "I recommend that everyone have a medical power of attorney, but only a few people need a general power of attorney," he said. "If you have a will, you can designate who will act as executor of your estate in probate."

To be more specific, Burger explained the different considerations that can go into choosing between an estate plan, a will, and a trust.

"A will provides a simple — and inexpensive — method of transferring ownership of your property. When **the value of your property exceeds the federal exemption, tax planning becomes a consideration**. Also, as the amount of your property increases, it sometimes makes sense to come up with more complicated designs to dispose of your assets. This creates a need for estate planning. Trusts also are used for estate planning and asset protection by individuals who operate businesses that can be sued."

In the case that a person has no assets, Burger said a will is still needed because most people have assets even if they do not acknowledge them. "There are very few people who truly have 'no assets.' A simple will is cheap insurance to make sure assets you have now or accumulate in the future will be disposed of as you wish and with minimal 'trauma' to your relatives."

That said, there are some important things to remember when putting together a will or creating an estate plan. Burger believes this can play a big part in making the situation a good one or a bad one for those left behind.

"Most people want to leave everything to their spouse, and if their spouse dies before them, to their children. Thought should be given to how this bequest to the children should be handled, especially if the children are minors," he noted. "There are many restrictions under Texas law on the rights of minors to control and manage property. Because of this, a testator who has minor children should give serious thought to who will act as guardian or custodian for the minor. Also, under the Probate Code, a guardianship of a minor ends when the minor turns 18. Many parents would not relish the thought of their 18-year-old child suddenly having control of a large sum of money. It is often better to create a testamentary trust that parcels out the money over a span of years to encourage children to attend college and become financially independent on their own."

Types of wills

There are different kinds of wills, depending on the purpose of the testator and state law limitations. The testator will have chosen the type he or she felt best met his or her specific needs. The will's format can vary depending on the testator's estate planning and who is intended to benefit in the will.

Although they need to be in writing and have these elements in common, not all wills look or sound alike. In addition to the personal quirks of the individuals who write them, different types of wills are drafted to suit specific purposes.

Mutual will: A testator prepares this type of will in conjunction with another person. For example: Sisters Cleo and Cora agree to support their disabled brother, Conrad, and Grandma Chloe. So, they decide that no matter who dies first, 40 percent of that first sister's estate goes to Conrad, 40 percent goes to Grandma Chloe, and the remaining 20 percent goes to other beneficiaries. When the second sister dies, 50 percent of her estate goes to Conrad, 20 percent goes to Grandma Chloe, and the remaining 30 percent goes to other beneficiaries. If Grandma Chloe dies before Cleo or Cora, her portion goes to Conrad. If Conrad dies before Cleo or Cora, his portion goes to Grandma Chloe.

Joint will: This is one will, that is, one legal document, for any two people, such a husband and wife. The problem with this kind of will is that it is irrevocable, which means it cannot be changed after one of the two parties dies. The reason is that both people must make all decisions. A lawyer can explain when this kind of will is a good idea, but most lawyers will suggest separate wills to avoid complications. Joint wills are not recognized in all states. A personal representative presented with one of these wills should consult an attorney about its validity.

Simple will: A single legal document written by one person that identifies who the testator is, who the beneficiaries are, the executor, the directions left for the care of people for whom the testator is responsible, and the distribution of assets is known as a simple will.

Holographic will: This special type of will does not require witnesses if it is written completely by hand and signed by the testator. It still must be clear that it is intended by the testator to be his or her will. Not all states recognize holographic wills. They are legal in Alaska, Arizona, Arkansas, California, Colorado, Idaho, Kentucky, Louisiana, Maine, Michigan, Mississippi, Montana, Nebraska, Nevada, New Jersey, North Carolina, North Dakota, Oklahoma, Pennsylvania, South Dakota, Tennessee, Texas, Utah, Virginia, West Virginia, and Wyoming.

Pour-over will: This will places some property into a trust that was established during the testator's lifetime (also called an inter vivos trust). The trust, in effect, is a beneficiary of the will.

Testamentary trust will: This will includes a provision that creates a trust and identifies the assets to be moved into the trust. *See Chapter 7 for more information on trusts.*

Nuncupative will: Also called an oral (spoken) will. As mentioned earlier, some states will allow this kind of will for limited purposes. Such a limited purpose will be a deathbed declaration and only cover personal property of little or no value. Some states recognize nuncupative wills for active military personnel or mariners at sea or for other persons conveying no more than $1,000 in personal property. This type of will is not useful to dispose of a complete estate.

Video will: In most cases, a will recorded on videotape or DVD will not be accepted as a legal document. Some states will, in extreme circumstances, allow a will to be recorded by a terminally ill person from a deathbed — literally. However, such a recording likely will be considered a nuncupative will and subject to the limitations of a nuncupative will.

Concerning Beneficiaries

The "traditional" child has been viewed to be the biological offspring of a married heterosexual couple. Otherwise, a child was considered illegitimate and likely to have limited, if any, legal rights as to the biological parents.

"Non-traditional" children are becoming more recognized in modern society. Over time, legally adopted children have become synonymous with biological children in the eyes of the law. But in an era when divorce, infertility, and same-sex couples mean children become part of a family through in vitro fertilization (IVF), adoptions originating in a foreign country, and stepchildren, inheritance rights can be complicated.

A child born outside a legally recognized union — in most states, this is defined as a marriage between a woman and a man, though this is changing — will automatically inherit her/his mother's estate unless disinherited by will. Inheritance from the biological father is not necessarily automatic.

Many state laws allow a child to inherit from a man who is identified as the father through a paternity test. The father also can marry the mother after the child is born and acknowledge himself as the father of the "out of wedlock" child. If a parental identity suit — the action taken to establish the biological relationship of an adult in a parent-child relationship — does not establish, the child's parent identity, then the child cannot inherit from the estate of the claimed parent.

So, who are legal children? Here are some ways to tell if a child is a legal child when preparing to distribute assents in a will:

☑ Stepchildren must be legally adopted by the stepparent to be considered part of a stepparent's family. If the stepparent did not formally adopt them and the stepparent's will directs his or her estate to fund trust funds or bequests for "my children," the stepchildren will not be included. Only those minors who are recognized by the state as lawful children will be entitled to that bequest. The stepparent might have thought of the non-adopted stepchildren as children to be covered by the trust, but legally they will not be entitled. If the stepparent had named the beneficiaries in the will by their proper names, e.g. "Jesse Jones, Julep

Jones, and Sondra Smith," then the issue of which are lawful children would not come up. They are identified by name, not by a "class" of persons as being the "children."

☑ A paternity test is the comparison of blood taken from the potential father against a blood sample of the child.

☑ A paternity suit is a legal action that is initiated to establish a man as the biological father of a child.

☑ While the question of parenthood is typically associated with the father, a parental identity test can be used to establish the biological relationship of a mother as well, such as in the case of abandonment, years of foster care, or other circumstances in which the identity of the biological mother, or a child, is not known.

Once a will is written, it is not etched in stone — it can be revised or even replaced. A new will replaces the old one either entirely or in part. The testator's intent about this ideally will be clear. The standard provision in this regard is "I revoke all prior wills and codicils" or something similar. If a testator intends to change only a part of a will, the better approach is to make a codicil, which is a separate legal document that adds to the existing will. It is written and executed with the same formalities as the original will but declares that it is a codicil and addresses only the change it is making. For example, in his will, Edward bequeathed his coin collection to James. Five years after making his will, Edward sells the coin collection. If he does not change the will and dies, there will be no coin collection, which would create an ademption situation. An ademption situation is a situation in which bequests in a will cannot be distributed because the bequest is no longer available.

Depending on the state law, James might be entitled to an equivalent from the estate or be out of luck. It certainly raises a question. Suppose no one but Edward knew he sold the coin collection and the whereabouts of the coin collection cannot be determined. Edward makes sure this confusion does not happen by writing a codicil to the will when he sells the coin collection. In the codicil, he makes clear the clause bequeathing to James is replaced by the codicil; he states that he no longer has the coin collection and that instead he bequeaths $5,000 to James, and that is all James shall receive under his will. Thus, Edward did not have to rewrite his entire will to fix the one provision. The codicil is an easy way to make a few simple changes without any confusion about the main document continuing as "the will." Even if James wants to challenge the codicil on some grounds, only the codicil — not the rest of the will — will be affected by the controversy.

If a beneficiary in a will dies before the testator, that it creates a lapsed gift. If the property exists and no contingent beneficiary is named, then the state steps in if it has an anti-lapse statute. The anti-lapse statute provides for who gets the bequest instead. If the state does not have such a statute, then the property would fall under the will's residuary clause. This is one of those situations where legal advice should be obtained to find out what the law requires.

Dying Intestate

Recall the sample will of Jason Little in the last chapter. What would have happened to Jason's property if he had not made a will and he died intestate? What would *not* have happened is distribution of anything to Charlie, The Perch Club of Lorain Scholarship Fund, or Thelma Goodbody. None of these were blood relatives of Jason in line to inherit in an intestate estate under Ohio law.

Every state has a statute that spells out who inherits from an intestate decedent, and the order in which inheritance rights are determined. The states are similar in this rule. They have a law called the statute of descent and distribution. Ohio's statute of descent and distribution is codified in Ohio Revised Code 2105.06 (as amended 1/13/2012), which provides that when a person dies intestate, his or her personal property shall be distributed and real property descend and pass according to the following order:

(A) If there is no surviving spouse, to the children of the intestate or their lineal descendants, per stirpes (Per stirpes is a legal term that means each branch of the family receives an equal share.)

(B) If there is a spouse and one or more children of the decedent or their lineal descendants surviving, and all of the decedent's children who survive or have lineal descendants surviving also are children of the surviving spouse, then the whole to the surviving spouse

(C) If there is a spouse and one child of the decedent or the child's lineal descendants surviving and the surviving spouse is not the natural or adoptive parent of the decedent's child, the first $20,000 plus one-half of the balance of the intestate estate to the spouse and the remainder to the child or the child's lineal descendants, per stirpes

(D) If there is a spouse and more than one child or their lineal descendants surviving, the first $60,000 if the spouse is the natural or adoptive parent of one, but not all, of the children, or the first $20,000 if the spouse is the natural or adoptive parent of none of the children, plus one-third of the balance of the intestate estate to the spouse and the remainder to the children equally, or to the lineal descendants of any deceased child, per stirpes

(E) If there are no children or their lineal descendants, then the whole to the surviving spouse

(F) If there is no spouse and no children or their lineal descendants, to the parents of the intestate equally, or to the surviving parent

(G) If there is no spouse, no children or their lineal descendants, and no parent surviving, to the brothers and sisters, whether of the whole or of the half blood of the intestate, or their lineal descendants, per stirpes

(H) If there are no brothers or sisters or their lineal descendants, one-half to the paternal grandparents of the intestate equally, or to the survivor of them, and one-half to the maternal grandparents of the intestate equally, or to the survivor of them

(I) If there is no paternal grandparent or no maternal grandparent, one-half to the lineal descendants of the deceased grandparents, per stirpes; if there are no such lineal descendants, then to the surviving grandparents or their lineal descendants, per stirpes; if there are no surviving grandparents or their lineal descendants, then to the next of kin of the intestate, provided there shall be no representation among the next of kin

(J) If there are no next of kin, to stepchildren or their lineal descendants, per stirpes

(K) If there are no stepchildren or their lineal descendants, escheat to the state

Whether a decedent has a will or is intestate, the estate's personal representative must locate and give notice of the estate to all next of kin or their lineal descendants. This is required because these persons have a right to make a claim on the estate. If the personal representative has no knowledge of any such persons, publication of the estate in the newspaper serves as notice to unknown persons, if they exist, to come forward and assert their claims. If they do not, their claims will be barred, similar to the creditors. In the case of Jason Little, Jason was not married when he died and he had no surviving spouse and no children or stepchildren. His parents and all his grandparents predeceased him and he had no siblings. If there were any descendants of Jason's grandparents, other than his own parents, Charlie could not find any evidence of them, and they did not come forward.

In short, Jason Little had no surviving heirs. Had Jason not made a will, his $60,000 (minus debts and expenses), his fishing gear, and his personal possessions would "escheat," which means that Jason's property would pass to the State of Ohio under section (K) of the statute. The law makes sure property will be distributed somewhere. The administrator of Jason's intestate estate would be required to sell Jason's physical possessions (i.e., the fishing gear and household items) so as to convert them to cash, and at the closing of the estate, the remaining money of several thousands of dollars would be paid out to the state of Ohio.

A hypothetical intestate estate such as this underscores rather dramatically the importance of having a will if it is important to a person where his or her property will go after death. Most married people assume, for example, that without a will, all they own automatically will pass to their spouse. This is true, though, only if the deceased has no children. False assumptions and un-expected results caused by an intestate situation showcases the importance of a will. A will not only expresses the desire of the testator but also makes the personal representative's job easier because in it the testator has given his or her representative a blueprint to follow.

Finding the beneficiaries

If there is a will, it will name the people who are entitled to the estate property after debts and taxes, if any, and costs of the estate are paid. The will may not include as beneficiaries all the persons who are entitled to inherit by law if there was no will. These people have a right to contest the will. An example is an existing surviving spouse who is not named in the will. Another example might be a child of the deceased who is not named when other children are. The point is, there are persons named by law who have a right of inheritance if there is no will or a will is invalid. All persons who have an interest in the estate must be notified that the estate has been opened so that they have the opportunity to assert any rights they believe they may have to all or part of the estate. It is the personal representative's responsibility to no-tify them, as well as all persons named as beneficiaries in the will.

What if the personal representative cannot locate such a per-son? People move. They change their names. They do not stay in touch with family. Even with the advent of the search capabilities of the Internet, people cannot always be located. As with notify-ing creditors, persons who might have a beneficial claim to an estate are notified by newspaper publication. This is legal notice because it is a public declaration of the estate. State law will pro-vide how long a "lost" beneficiary has to make his or her claim to the estate.

The Living Will or Advance Health Care Directive

Some issues that were once traditionally mentioned in a person's last will and testament are now covered by most people in another will that has become part of estate planning: the living will or advance health care directive. In some states, this takes the form of a durable health care power of attorney. Wishes such as organ donation, donation of one's body to science, and funeral directives, often written out in traditional wills, were difficult to carry out, if at all, due to the lapse of time from death until the will was found and read. Now, for these situations, we have advance health care directives.

Advance health care directives, in whatever form they take and depending on state law, usually name an alternative decision-maker for situations in which a person cannot speak due to a medical condition. Even with the clear terms of the advance care directive, someone generally is designated as the person's surrogate. For continuity in estate planning, a testator might name the same person for this purpose as is named the estate's personal representative in the last will and testament. As well, a person who dies intestate may have had an advance health care directive in place.

Even if the estate's personal representative was not informed about an advance health care directive, decisions relating to the deceased's final illness and death pursuant to an advance health care directive could have legal implications that must be addressed by the estate. For example, were the testator's wishes observed as set forth in the advance health care directive? If not, there could be medical bills for unauthorized procedures charged to the estate that should be contested, as well as possible other legal claims on behalf of the deceased. Conversely, did the testator specify certain lifesaving measures be done that were not carried out? In this case, the estate's personal representative would have a legal obligation to investigate a wrongful death claim. For these reasons, a personal representative should know something about advance health care directives, whether deceased had an advance health care directive and if so, whether its provisions were in any way relevant to the death. However, for many of these complicated situations, you might need to enlist the help of a lawyer.

The point of the advance health care directive is to declare what kind of lifesaving measures are wanted — or not — by a person if he or she becomes incapacitated and unable to express his or her wishes at the time. All states now recognize a form of living wills, advance health care directives, or durable power of attorney for health care, but the documents are not uniform. Some states will only allow living wills to apply to a person who is permanently unconscious or has a terminal illness. Others will allow them for advanced-stage illnesses such as the final stages of Alzheimer's, when death is not imminent.

An advance health care directive should be specific and address the person's medical history, and clearly state the person's wishes for withholding life-saving measures. For example, if a person has a history of congestive heart failure in the family and has been diagnosed with the same condition but does not want extraordinary measures — such as being kept alive by feeding tube or respirator — used to prolong his or her life, that wish needs to be spelled out.

Another way to make sure such wishes are followed regarding medical care is to designate a health care power of attorney (HCPA), also known as a medical power of attorney. A HCPA involves designating another person to make medical decisions for a person when he or she cannot. Many states have laws that allow family members to make some or all of a person's health care decisions. A durable power of attorney also can be used to give someone else the authority to make medical decisions by including the health care provisions as part of the document. This kind of power of attorney allows an authorized person to act on behalf of the grantor of that power of attorney. The "durable" nature of the document means that its power survives if the grantor is incompetent to express his or her wishes, such as being in a coma.

Making decisions about life-sustaining treatment, artificial nutrition and hydration, and organ donation are the type of advanced health care directives most people prepare. Many people are now preparing these documents online. If an estate representative needs a copy of the deceased's advance health care directive and a copy is not readily available from family or medical sources, online sources are a place to look.

CASE STUDY: MYDIRECTIVES.COM

L. Scott Brown, president
ADVault, Inc.
17304 Preston Road, Suite 800
Dallas, Texas 75252
info@MyDirectives.com
www.MyDirectives.com

Unexpected end-of-life situations can happen at any age, so all adults, not just the ill or elderly, need advance medical directives. Although you probably know how you feel about end-of-life issues, there may come a time in the future when you are seriously injured or too ill to be able to make or communicate decisions about medical treatment for yourself. In such a situation, advance medical directives provide a record of your wishes so that your family and doctors have a guide in making medical treatment decisions on your behalf that are consistent with your values, beliefs, and preferences.

MyDirectives® is a free Web-based service that allows you to securely create and update your own Universal Advance Digital Directive (uADD)™ online. Depending on how prepared you are and how many questions your state or country requires, it usually takes between 15 minutes and an hour to complete your uADD in the system. Your directive is encrypted and stored in the secure MyDirectives database and is available to you and your medical treatment providers (usually hospital admissions staff, emergency room nurses, and doctors) 24 hours a day, seven days a week. No information about you is available to anyone, including the hospital, until you've digitally signed your uADD. Once that happens, your uADD is available to be viewed and downloaded by an authorized medical facility, but nobody can change any information in the file except you.

The advantage of complete information available instantly to an authorized medical provider is compelling in situations like Kay's story. In a routine mammogram, Kay was diagnosed with an aggressive form of cancer. Kay had no living will, no health care power of attorney, in place. The need for quick surgery and treatment decisions left little time for her to consider alternatives for care in "what if" situations. Gowned for surgery with an IV stuck in her arm, Kay was faced with decisions such as if she wanted to be cremated or buried, if she wanted to have an autopsy, if she wanted to donate organs, if she wanted certain measures of life support. She was so in shock, so emotionally bombarded by the whole experience — the diagnosis, the enormity of the events facing her, the reaction of her family — that she could hardly come up with answers. Kay literally was being wheeled down the hall to the operating room while she called back to her sister that if anything happened to her that day she wanted to be buried next to their grandfather.

Having thought out these choices in advance and put them in place in an easily retrievable legal document would have relieved both Kay and her family of the need for rushed, painful decisions at the most traumatic point of life's moments. MyDirectives' online system simplifies the process and provides ready support for you.

Availability of your directive through electronic access also alleviates the need to locate documents and produce them to the medical providers who require them. A complete, thorough document will not be helpful if it cannot be found.

Once you're admitted to a medical facility, and you either hand your advance medical directive to the hospital admitting staff or give them permission to access it from the MyDirectives database, the hospital will attach the printed document to your medical record. Hospitals will see your signed advance medical directives, any answers you give in the My Thoughts section, and a summary sheet with contact information and data about your signed documents. Medical facilities can search and print your records if you're being admitted to a facility and you ask them to, or if you can't communicate your wishes, the admitting staff person, nurse, or doctor can go to the MyDirectives database and look for your uADD. Insurance companies cannot access the information you've stored in MyDirectives.

We are pleased that our system has been endorsed by such major facilities as Baylor Health Care System, Plano, Texas. Your Universal Advance Digital Directive in **MyDirectives.com** is a legal document, and we take the position that it should be enforceable, but we can't guarantee that every medical treatment provider in every jurisdiction throughout the world will follow it.

Although a person's medical information is private by law, the estate personal representative has legal authority to obtain all medical records of the deceased, including an advance health care directive. Such records might be necessary to investigate and resolve potential claims by or against the estate. This is one of the many estate management obligations that can arise in the course of wrapping up the deceased's affairs.

Chapter 5

Estate Management Obligations

*a*s you have seen in the previous chapters, the personal representative has several duties and responsibilities to execute for the decedent's estate. Most of these revolve around accounting for property and money owed. In this chapter, we will talk about how you find all the pieces of the estate to count as assets and any other estate management obligations you will need to fulfill before moving on to the debts of the estate.

Taking Inventory

As you saw with the sample procedure in Chapter 3, one of the first of the primary duties of the personal representative is to marshal the estate's assets. What are they? Where are they? The following sections talk about the types of assets you are likely to encounter in the estate.

First, you should know the difference between probate property and non-probate property. When settling an estate, probate property refers to property that will go through the estate before passing on to the beneficiaries. Non-probate property is automatically

passed on to the beneficiaries without needing to be part of the estate or having any effect on the value of the estate. For example, real property owned solely by the decedent, bank accounts owned solely by the decedent, and tangible property belonging to the decedent all would be considered probate property; it is up to you as the executor to find this property, inventory it, and pass it along to the appropriate beneficiaries. However, real property owned equally by two or more people, life insurance payouts, and other trusts and accounts might legally pass immediately to their proper beneficiaries with no action on the part of an estate. You will see an example of this in the joint ownership with right of survivorship deed in the first section.

Real property

Real property is exactly what it sounds like: property such as land or a house on land that is owned by the decedent. However, whether such property is part of the estate can be questionable when more than one person claims ownership of the property.

Real property is most commonly transferred outside of probate by a specific deed mechanism called a joint ownership with right of survivorship deed. This arrangement allows people to own property together and have it pass automatically to the surviving owner(s) when one of the owners named on the deed dies. This is a concept similar to joint ownership of bank accounts where more than one person is named as a joint owner on the bank account with right of survivorship; the balance of the account passes immediately and automatically to the surviving owner when the other person on the account dies. In both cases, the transfer of ownership occurs outside of probate.

Most states permit joint ownership of real property with right of survivorship. In this situation, the real property will not be part of the probate estate because the probate process is not needed to oversee the transfer. The law has provided another way to do it.

If the decedent was an owner of real estate without a survivorship arrangement, though, then the property will be part of the probate estate. The estate's personal representative will have the responsibility of managing the property until it is either sold or transferred to a beneficiary of the estate. In the case of rental properties, for example, the personal representative will be responsible for rent collection and property maintenance. The estate representative uses the assets of the estate to cover the costs of such maintenance.

The personal representative also might need to supervise and manage the sale of real estate. The proceeds from the sale then become cash assets of the estate. A sale might be necessitated by instructions in the will, liquidation to satisfy payment of debts, agreement of the beneficiaries of the estate who have an interest in the real estate, or order of the court as part of the court's resolution in a contested action involving the real estate. The court will have specific forms for the personal representative to use in these situations. (In the management of probate administration, there is a form for everything.) Every court will have its own form. *Samples of forms from specific state courts, for illustrative purpose, are included in this book's Appendix D.* You will be responsible for getting the required forms in your case from your own court. Whether the personal representative will have the power to sell real estate without first obtaining an order from the court depends on the powers conferred in the will and the rules of the specific court.

Another concern when dealing with real property as part of the estate is property insurance. As you begin compiling accounts and inventorying the estate, make sure to document and contact the property insurance provider for any property that is part of the estate. As with other accounts in the estate, you will want to change the account name into the estate's name instead of the decedent's so that you will have the authority to make changes to the account. Many insurance companies will insist upon a new policy if you make this change. You can pay for the insurance renewal or maintenance from the assets of the estate. *Estate expenses will be covered in the next chapter.* Once the real property has passed into the hands of the beneficiary, he or she will be in charge of insuring the property from that point forward.

Ancillary proceedings

Another wrinkle about the probate of real estate might arise when the decedent owned real estate in another state that did not pass on death by a joint ownership with right of survivorship deed. In order for the real estate to be transferred lawfully in that other state, the personal representative will need to arrange for what is called ancillary probate, which is a secondary proceeding in the courts of the state where the real estate is located. An order of the ancillary probate court in the state where the real estate is located is necessary to have the ownership transferred to the beneficiary of the will or the legal heir of the decedent if there is no will. In this situation, the personal representative is well advised to obtain legal counsel in the other state to handle this necessary ancillary proceeding. The estate is responsible for paying the costs of this action.

Some states will accept your letters of authority from your court to be sufficient for the ancillary proceeding. For example, Jon is the executor of his father's estate in Ohio. Dad, who was a widower when he died, was the sole owner of a parcel of real estate in Indiana. Dad left the real estate to Jon's brother, George. Because an Ohio court does not have jurisdiction — the power and

control — over the Indiana real estate, Jon needs to file an ancillary proceeding in the Indiana court in the county where the real estate is located. Fortunately, Indiana will recognize Jon's letters of authority issued to him by the Ohio court. Jon can have a copy of his Ohio probate court papers appointing him executor and a copy of the will filed with the Indiana probate court of the county where the real estate is located. Then he will be able to have the property transferred to George. Nevertheless, Jon would be smart to get assistance from an Indiana lawyer in that county to be sure the local procedures are followed correctly and to expedite the process.

Ancillary proceedings add time and expense to probate administration, but they need not be something to fear. Even when getting the assistance of legal counsel, you can minimize your cost by having an understanding of the procedure.

Personal property

Other property that might be a part of the estate includes automobiles, other vehicles, trailers, collectibles, family heirlooms, furniture, cash, bank accounts, stocks, bonds, money market accounts, and household goods. All these items and their value must be listed as part of the probate estate inventory, as you saw in Chapter 3. Property is classified as tangible (physical items you can touch and distribute "in kind," such as coins, antiques, books, furniture, and cars) and intangible (money and its paper equivalent such as stocks and bonds, and symbolic concepts of value such as trademarks, patents, copyrights, and business good will).

The decedent might have owned items of special value that are part of the estate's assets. These will need to be itemized on the inventory, authenticated, and appraised.

To determine if an intangible property exists, you will need to contact institutions that hold the decedent's accounts. On the top of this list should be the decedent's bank. Once again, double and triple check for safety deposit boxes the decedent could have placed valuables or other statements for safekeeping.

Intangible property also can include pensions, profit sharing, annuities, and deferred compensation, as well as any life insurance or other kinds of insurance that affect the value of the estate. These might not be probate assets depending on how they were set up, but you might be able to include them in the estate's value. If the estate itself is named the beneficiary in these types of property, these proceeds are probate property and should be included in the estate. Make sure you read each item carefully so you know how to proceed. With life insurance, make sure you find and contact the source of the decedent's life insurance if he or she had a policy. This life insurance could be used to pay off some of the medical bills and funeral expenses, depending on the policy. For the most part, however, life insurance is considered non-probate property and thus will not have much effect on the value of the estate.

If the decedent's records include appraisals for insurance, purchase invoices, or similar lists of valuation, these will be helpful, but unless they are current, a new appraisal will be necessary for present value. Appraisal is necessary because all the estate's assets must be totaled to determine if estate tax or inheritance tax obligations are triggered for the estate. Examples of the types of unique collections that one might find in an estate include:

- Guns
- Coins
- Rare stamps
- Vintage or celebrity clothing
- Baseball cards
- Sports memorabilia
- Music boxes
- Figurines or statuary from a specific company and production line, such as, for example: Delft, Lladró®, Gorham®, Hummel®, Dresden, Royal Doulton®
- Dolls
- Snuffboxes
- Japanese netsukes
- China sets
- Sterling silver sets
- Oriental carpets
- Rare antique photos
- Rare books
- Antique furniture pieces
- Paintings

This non-exhaustive list suggests that any collection could have value and should not be discounted. Only an expert can say whether a collection is valuable. Most probate courts have lists of appraisers from which you can select someone to value special items of the estate. Some courts might require court approval of the appraiser before the appraisal is done. Appraisers are not usually difficult to locate. Local museums and dealers in the type of property in question are places to start. Professional auctioneers can be helpful as well.

After viewing the assets of the estate and recording the values of each in the inventory, you might decide you need to enlist the help of a CPA to assist with determining the taxes involved in the estate or other accounting issues.

The following worksheet is useful for creating an initial inventory list before preparing the court's inventory form. *You also can find an editable copy on the CD-ROM with this book.*

DECEDENT'S PROPERTY AS OF DATE OF DEATH

Item Classification and Item Name	ID No. or Description	Location	Estimated Value @ Date of Death	Appraised Value/ Appraiser/ Appraisal Date	Notes
Real property					
Stocks, bonds					
Bank accounts, CDs, money markets, etc.					
Vehicles, boats, trailers					

Item Classification and Item Name	ID No. or Description	Location	Estimated Value @ Date of Death	Appraised Value/ Appraiser/ Appraisal Date	Notes
Notes, debts owed decedent					
Cash					
Insurance, annuities					
Collectibles					
Animals, livestock					

Item Classification and Item Name	ID No. or Description	Location	Estimated Value @ Date of Death	Appraised Value/ Appraiser/ Appraisal Date	Notes
Jewelry					
Furniture/ household goods					
Other property					

Estate Income

The estate might derive income during the time it is pending in probate. This is income that arises after the decedent's death during the pendency of the estate. Such income includes rent from rental properties that are part of the probate estate and interest paid on funds on deposit in financial accounts. You need to keep track of and account for such income.

As seen in the fictional example of an estate in Chapter 3, the first thing you should do to keep track of this income is to open a bank account in the name of the estate. This can be at the bank where the decedent kept his or her accounts, or it can be at a bank of your choosing. This step gives you the authority to make decisions on behalf of the estate. Once you have a bank account set up for the estate, you will be able to see the estate income more easily and keep track of the estate expenses, which are covered in the next chapter.

Estate income equal to or exceeding $600 is reportable and taxed. IRS Form 1041 is used for this tax. *A copy of the form is provided in this book's Appendix D, along with other pertinent tax forms.* Federal forms are also available at **www.IRS.gov.** Income becomes part of the estate's assets.

ESTATE INCOME AND DEPOSITS

Type	Date Received	Name of Payor	Description of Expense	Amount	Comment Notes
Rent					
Sale					
Interest					

Type	Date Received	Name of Payor	Description of Expense	Amount	Comment Notes
Dividends					
Debt paid (owed to decedent)					
Other					

As stated before, the greatest part of the personal representative's duties is consumed in managing and accounting for property, whether it is itemizing, finding, safekeeping, spending, or distributing. *The next chapter takes a closer look at spending obligations – creditors' claims and estate expenses.*

Chapter 6

Debts of the Estate and Estate Expenses

*F*rom the date of the decedent's death until the final settlement of the estate, the personal representative must assess any debts owed by the decedent and any immediate or ongoing bills to be paid. To do this, the personal representative must take steps to contact any creditors who could have claims to some of the estate's assets. Assessing which creditors' claims should be paid and how much they should be paid is the personal representative's responsibility.

Issuing Notice to Creditors

Part of the personal representative's duty prescribed in the probate procedure is to issue notice to known and unknown creditors of the estate. Time limits are prescribed by state statute as to how long a creditor has to make a claim to the estate. *A table included in this chapter* summarizes these time limits by state, with the state statute reference provided, so you can check for changes in your state.

When you are issued appointment papers from the court (e.g. "Letters of Authority") designating you as the estate's personal representative, you then provide the written notice to creditors that the estate is filed, and they are on notice to file their claims. You will know some creditors from bills that have been mailed to the decedent by name. Even if you have such bills, however, you need to write to those creditors by regular mail (unless another means of direct delivery is required by statute) to identify yourself as the estate's representative and request written verification of the amount the creditor claims to be owed. *A sample letter written by hypothetical representative, Charles Lightfoot, is included in Chapter 3. An additional example is included in Appendix C of this book.*

In addition, you will be required to publish a public notice to creditors in the local newspaper. Most states will provide the language to use in this notice. In Virginia, a court commissioner issues the notice. The notice is done by publication in a local newspaper of general circulation in the county where the estate is being probated so all potential creditors are on notice that the estate has been filed and that they need to make their claim to the estate. With both forms of notice — direct letter and publication — the creditor then has a specified period under the law to make the creditor's claim to the estate. If the creditor fails to make a claim within the prescribed time limit, the claim is barred and the estate is not obligated to pay it. An exception is the decedent's funeral/burial costs, which must be paid before the estate can be closed, as must taxes and attorney and representative fees.

Funeral Arrangements

The funeral is nearly always completed before the court appointment of the personal representative. An exception might arise when the body is held for examination by a coroner or the funeral service is delayed following a cremation. Law requires funeral expenses to be paid first in settling an estate. Whether you are directly involved in handling the funeral arrangements, as personal representative you will need to prove to the court that all funeral expenses are satisfied and that no outstanding claim for them is held against the estate, either by the funeral provider or by any person who paid the bill. Submitting a paid receipt from the funeral provider to the court will constitute sufficient proof. If someone other than the estate (or the decedent as a prepaid service) paid the funeral bill, that person will need to be reimbursed by the estate or submit an affidavit that he or she waives and forever relinquishes any claim to reimbursement of the fees.

Publication

As mentioned above, it is nearly always the responsibility of the personal representative to publish public notice of the estate for creditors. The state's probate law prescribes how this notice by publication should be done. Most courts provide a form, or the language to use, for this purpose. Publication means placing a notice in a local newspaper of general circulation. Most often, this will be a newspaper published within the same county as the decedent's residence, nearly always the county in which the estate is being probated. When the notice appears in a newspaper, containing the information prescribed for such notice, creditors are deemed "notified" that they must present their claims to the estate's personal representative. Usually publication is repeated over a specified period, such as a running notice for three consecutive weeks.

Although state law varies as to the precise type and wording of the notice, a typical creditors' notice will include: decedent's name, last residence address, and date of death. Other information that might be required includes whether a will has been submitted to probate, the date of the will's execution, and the statement that the estate will be distributed to the beneficiaries. The notice also will state that unless claims are submitted according to law, they will be forever barred. Creditors are expected to know the time limits pertaining to their claims, or to ascertain them, or the time limit might be stated in the notice. The estate pays the cost of publishing the creditors' notice.

Following is a sample creditors' notice by publication for a then-pending estate in Alabama, published in the *Jacksonville News*, for three consecutive weeks: January 5, 12, and 19, 2010. *A sample court form for notice by publication to creditors also is included in this book's Appendix C.*

"NOTICE TO CREDITORS STATE OF ALABAMA CALHOUN COUNTY PROBATE COURT CASE NO. 29611 IN THE MATTER OF THE ESTATE OF REINALODO ANTONIO BOYD, DECEASED
Location: Jacksonville 36265

NOTICE TO CREDITORS STATE OF ALABAMA CALHOUN COUNTY PROBATE COURT CASE NO. 29611 IN THE MATTER OF THE ESTATE OF REINALODO ANTONIO BOYD, DECEASED Letters Testamentary on the estate of REINALODO ANTONIO BOYD, deceased, having been granted to ROOSEVELT BOYD JR., the undersigned on December 16, 2009, by the Honorable Alice K. Martin, Judge of Probate of said County, notice is hereby given that all persons having claims against said estate, are hereby required to present the same within the time allowed by law, or the same will be barred. ROOSEVELT BOYD JR., of the Last Will and Testament of REINALODO ANTONIO BOYD, Deceased. Alice K. Martin Judge of Probate Jacksonville News Calhoun Co., AL January 5, 12, 19, 2010."

The personal representative is responsible for publishing the notice in accordance with the court procedure and filing certification of notice with the court. The personal representative should also maintain copies, with newspaper clippings of the notice (including newspaper masthead and dates) in his or her own file.

Direct notice

Similarly, as also mentioned, the personal representative will send direct notices to known creditors. Copies of the actual, individual notices mailed out should be kept in the personal representative's file. Unless the probate court or state law requires a specific type of mail, such as certified mail, it is recommended that notices be sent with, at minimum, a Certificate of Mailing issued by the post office to show that a piece of mail has been placed in the U.S. Postal System to a specific address on a specific date. This provides evidence for the personal representative's file that the notice was mailed to the creditor as of a date certain. The personal representative then keeps a copy of the letter sent with the Certificate of Mailing. The date mailed is important because, in many states, that date starts the time limitation period in which the creditor must respond with his or her claim.

Additionally, many of the decedent's debts, such as credit card balances, might be negotiable, that is, the credit card company might accept a lesser amount, such as 80 percent of the balance due, or less, to have the claim paid off and closed. When you have the most recent bill from the credit card company, write a letter to the company identifying yourself as the estate representative. Include a copy of your letters of authority or court order appointing you as the estate representative and a copy of the decedent's death certificate. In your letter, state that you are prepared to settle the account on behalf of the estate and request a company representative with authority to discuss the account contact you. Provide the telephone number you want the company to use to contact you and your mailing address on your letter heading. When the company representative calls, ask how much the company could discount the bill to get the matter closed as soon as possible. If you are able to reach an agreement on the phone, ask the representative to fax you a letter immediately stating the amount the company will take to fully settle and close the account. Do not send money to this or any creditor who agrees to settle for less than the total amount claimed without first getting the agreement in writing.

A personal representative is not personally liable to creditors for the estate's debts. However, a personal representative might be held personally liable to the estate for paying illegitimate claims or claims that are time-barred because by paying those claims, the personal representative has improperly spent estate assets that would otherwise be available to distribute to the estate's beneficiaries or to pay legitimate creditors. Also, in many states, a personal representative could be held personally liable to creditors who properly make their claims to the estate but are not paid. Make sure you know your state's time limitations and laws regarding when creditors must be paid.

Time Limitations for Filing Creditor Claims

The time limitations period for filing creditor claims with a decedent's estate vary by state. In some states, you will note, there is a dual limitation period: one based on the notice issued to creditors and a longer one in which no notice is given, as might happen if no estate is filed, such as when a person dies with few, if any, probate assets.

Note that it is the creditor's obligation to make the claim to the estate. For this reason, the personal representative should not automatically pay off debts based solely on documentation in the decedent's records. For one thing, that amount might not be correct. Second, if the creditor does not properly submit his or her claim to the estate upon the notice and within the time limit required by law, the estate will not be obliged to pay it. The personal representative's prime obligation is to conserve the estate assets, not voluntarily pay claims that might not be valid or that are not properly submitted by the creditor for payment.

A time-barred claim is one that is too old to be collected lawfully. An example would be a personal injury claim for something allegedly caused by the decedent several years before he or she died. Most personal injury claims become void if not made within a couple of years of the injury; the express time limit varies by state, but the point is to make sure claims are made in a timely fashion, are legitimate, and are correct in the amount claimed. Another example is a medical bill that already has been paid by the decedent's health insurance or Medicare. Medical bills do not always reflect insurance payments if they were issued before all insurance payments have been made by the insurance companies. You need to be sure all insurance coverage has been correctly applied to medical bills. Here, too, the medical provider — doctor or hospital, for example — might be willing to negotiate a final settlement of the bill for less than the amount stated on the billing statement. Another time-barred claim is one that comes in from a creditor after the statutory claims period for creditors to bring their claims has expired.

The following table contains the time limitations for creditors' estate claims for all 50 states with the corresponding state law provisions. Always check state law to see if there have been any changes in the requirement.

TIME LIMITATIONS FOR CREDITORS TO BRING CLAIMS TO PROBATE ESTATE

STATE	TIME LIMITATION(S)	STATE STATUTE
Alabama	6 months after appointment of personal representative or 5 months from first publication date of notice, whichever is later. Creditor receiving actual notice has 30 days after such notice.	ALA Code 43-2-350
Alaska	4 months after first date of publication of notice; 3 years after death if no notice	AS 13.16.450, 460
Arizona	4 months after first date of publication of notice or 60 days after actual notice, whichever is later	AZ Code 14-3801

STATE	TIME LIMITATION(S)	STATE STATUTE
Arkansas	6 months after first publication of notice to creditors	AK Code 28-50-101
California	4 months after date of appointment of personal representative or 60 days after actual notice	CA Probate Code 9100
Colorado	4 months after first publication date if notice published; otherwise 1 year from decedent's death	CRS 15-12-801, 803
Connecticut	150 days after appointment of first personal representative	Connecticut Code 45a-356
Delaware	8 months after decedent's death	Del. Code 12-2102
District of Columbia	6 months after first publication notice	DC Statute 20-903
Florida	3 months after first notice by publication or 30 days after actual notice; 2 years after death if no notice	FL Statute 733.702, 710
Georgia	6 months after court's qualification of first personal representative	OCGA 53-7-42
Hawaii	4 months after first notice by publication or 60 days after actual notice, whichever is later	Hawaii Code 560:3-801
Idaho	4 months after first publication of notice or 60 days after actual notice, whichever is later. If no notice given, 3 years after decedent's date of death	Idaho Statute 15-3-801, 803
Illinois	6 months after first date of publication of notice or 3 months after actual notice, whichever is later	ILCS 5/18-3
Indiana	3 months after the date of the first published notice to creditors or 3 months after the court has revoked probate of a will; otherwise, 9 months after date of decedent's death	IC 29-1-14-1
Iowa	4 months after the date of the second publication of the notice to creditors or, as to each claimant whose identity is reasonably ascertainable, 1 month after service of notice by ordinary mail to the claimant's last known address	Iowa Code 633.410
Kansas	4 months after notice of personal representative to creditors	Kansas Statute 59-1302
Kentucky	6 months after appointment of personal representative; otherwise, 2 years after decedent's death	KRS 396.011
Louisiana	3 months after date of decedent's death	CCP 3302
Maine	4 months after first date of publication of notice	Maine Revised Statute 3-801

STATE	TIME LIMITATION(S)	STATE STATUTE
Maryland	Earlier of: 4 months after date of decedent's death or 2 months after actual notice from personal representative	MCA 7-103
Massachusetts	1 year after date of decedent's death	MA Probate Code 3-803
Michigan	4 months after date of publication of notice, or later of 4 months after publication or 30 days after receipt of actual notice after personal representative (if creditor known to personal representative during 4-month publication period); otherwise, if no notice, 3 years after date of decedent's death	MCL 700-3803
Minnesota	1 year after date of decedent's death	MN Probate code 524.3-803
Mississippi	90 days after personal representative's first notice to creditors	MS Code 91-7-151
Missouri	6 months after the date of the first published notice of letters testamentary or of administration or, if notice was actually mailed to, or served upon, such creditor, within 2 months after the date such notice was mailed, or served, whichever is later	MO Statute 473.360
Montana	4 months after first published notice by personal representative or 30 days after actual notice, whichever is later	MCA 72-3-801
Nebraska	4 months after notice; otherwise, 3 years after death of decedent	Nebraska Statute 30-2485
Nevada	90 days after first publication of notice by personal representative or 30 days after actual notice to creditor, whichever is later	NRS 147.040
New Hampshire	6 months after appointment of personal representative; for insolvent estates, 6 months after appointment of commissioner(s) to manage claims	NHS 556:1 (claims against personal representative) NHS 557:7 (insolvent estate)
New Jersey	9 months after death of decedent	NJ Statute 3B:22-4
New Mexico	2 months after published notice or 2 months after actual notice, whichever is later	NM Code 45-3-801
New York	After publication of notice or 7 months from issuing of letters testamentary or of administration to personal representative	NY EPT Law 11-1.5(a)
North Carolina	3 months from date of first publication or mailing of notice	GS 28A-14-1(a)
North Dakota	3 months after mailing notice to creditors that are known to the personal representative and after first publication of notice or within 3 years after decedent's death if notice to creditors has not been published and mailed	NDCC 30.1-19-01 & 30.1-19-03

STATE	TIME LIMITATION(S)	STATE STATUTE
Ohio	6 months after death of decedent	ORC 2117.06
Oklahoma	2 months after date of first publication or after mailing notice to known creditors	Okla. Statute 58, Section 331
Oregon	4 months after date of first publication or 30 days after mailing of notice to known creditors	ORS 115.005
Pennsylvania	1 year after first public notice of death of decedent	PA Code 3385
Rhode Island	6 months after date of qualification of personal representative	RI Code 33-11-5.1
South Carolina	8 months from publication of notice or 60 days from actual notice, whichever is later; otherwise, 1 year from date of decedent's death if no notice	SC 62-3-801, 803
South Dakota	Date set in notice by publication to unknown creditors, in written notice mailed to known creditors or as to all creditors, 3 years from date of decedent's death	SD 29A-3-803
Tennessee	4 months after receipt of notice	Tenn. Code Ann. 30-2-317(a) (1)-(4).
Texas	4 months after receipt of notice	Texas Probate Code 294
Utah	3 months after first publication of notice to creditors; for written notice to known creditors, 90 days after first publication date or 60 days from mailing or delivery of notice, whichever is later	Utah Uniform Probate Code 75-3-801
Vermont	4 months after first publication of notice to creditors; 3 years from decedent's death if no publication done	14 V.S.A. § 1203
Virginia	1 year after publication creditor notice	VA Code 64.1-158.
Washington	4 months after publication of creditor notice or 30 days after actual creditor notice; otherwise, 24 months from death if no notice	RCW 11.40.05
West Virginia	90 days after first publication of creditor notice	WV Code 44-1-14a
Wisconsin	3 to 4 months after court order is issued giving upon application for administration, exact date set by court; 1 year from date of decedent's death if no notice given	Wis. Code 859.01, 859.48
Wyoming	3 months after creditor notice; 2 years from date of decedent's death if no estate filed	WY Probate Code 2-7-201 & 2-4-212

Resolving Creditor Claims

As mentioned, the personal representative only should entertain claims properly made to the estate within the statutory time limitation. When a claim is made in a timely manner, it still must be evaluated for validity and correctness of the amount claimed. If a dispute arises regarding a claim, either by you or one of the estate's beneficiaries, attempt to resolve the matter with the creditor directly. If you are unsuccessful, or if you have any questions about the creditor's claim, file the unresolved objections to a creditor's claim with the court for determination and approval of the amount to be paid.

Reasons why you might reject a creditor's claim include:

- The claim was previously paid by decedent. You might find in the decedent's records a paid receipt, correspondence, or a canceled check that indicates the claim was paid, or a surviving spouse or other relative might claim the bill was paid.

- The creditor did not actually supply the services or products (or product was returned). Correspondence or other documents in the decedent's papers might evidence this, or you are able to determine by inspection of property that the claimed service was not done.

- The creditor's services or products were defective. Again, there might be evidence that the decedent had already disputed this creditor's services or product, or you might discover for yourself that there is a problem.

- Someone else paid the bill for decedent. An example would be a medical bill paid by medical insurance.

- The creditor's claim is time-barred. The creditor did not make the claim within the required time for the estate or is foreclosed by another statute of limitations imposed by law.

- The claim was the subject of an active, unresolved dispute between the decedent and the creditor in an action such as a mediation or litigation, at the time of decedent's death.

- Additionally, there might be improper service charges or interest appended to a debt. Be careful about these. Even if they seem "routine" on their face, creditors will often remove them if you ask, to expedite getting their money.

Paying the claims

If you do not object to a claim that is filed within the proper time, you might pay it from the estate funds. If there are insufficient funds in the estate to pay all valid claims, you will have to consider the priority of claims that are payable by an estate according to your state's law. Although you need to know what your state precisely requires in this situation, the following is a typical order of priority in which claims are paid:

1. Cost to administer the estate: Included here are court costs, fees, and expenses owed to personal representative, bond premiums, attorney fees, appraiser fees, and fees for other professionals engaged to assist the estate administration.

2. Funeral costs: Many courts will require a paid receipt from the funeral services provider.

3. Federal taxes: The decedent's personal income tax owed at time of death and estate tax (if any). *Taxes will be discussed further in Chapter 9.*

4. Decedent's medical and hospital charges incurred immediately before death (also referenced as decedent's last or final illness). Note that charges deemed excessive, or unsupported by itemized dates and description of services provided, can (and should) be challenged as "unreasonable."

5. State taxes. Decedent's personal income tax owed at time of death and estate and/or inheritance tax (if any)

6. Other claims

The following chart can be used to help organize debts of the estate:

DEBTS OF DECEDENT

Debt Description	Sole or Joint Debt - Describe	Creditor's Name Address Contact Name Phone	Amount at Date of Death	Date(s) & Type of Notice Sent Creditor	Creditor Claim Deadline	Date Paid	Notes
Funeral expenses							
Real estate mortgage(s)							
Car/other vehicle loans							
Credit cards							

Debt Description	Sole or Joint Debt - Describe	Creditor's Name Address Contact Name Phone	Amount at Date of Death	Date(s) & Type of Notice Sent Creditor	Creditor Claim Deadline	Date Paid	Notes
Taxes							
Other debts							

Estate expenses

The estate also will have expenses that arise as part of its administration, for example, the court costs for filing and processing the estate. If real estate must be managed during the estate's administration, there likely will be costs associated with that, such as repairs and maintenance (e.g., changing locks, insurance, lawn care, utilities). Attorney fees, appraiser fees, and executor/administrator fees also are estate expenses. If an ancillary proceeding is necessitated in another state for transfer of real estate, the cost of that proceeding, including legal fees, is an estate expense. In short, whatever must be expended to administer the estate is an estate expense.

The easiest way to go about paying these expenses is to open a bank account in the estate's name, as seen in the fictional example in Chapter 3. You will need to supply the bank with your letter of authority so that you have full authority to run the estate account. You then can transfer much of the monetary assets of the estate into this bank account, and then use the estate checkbook to pay for these estate expenses. Remember to keep very good track of your receipts and expenses because you might need to show the court your documentation and reasoning for why you made the purchases you did.

The form below, designed to itemize estate expenses, lists several types of expenses that might be incurred in the course of handling an estate. The following worksheet is useful to keep track of estate expenses. Receipts and all records of transactions must be kept. You can organize yourself in various ways. If you keep your worksheet on your computer, you can keep a handwritten draft attached to a file folder in which you keep the receipts. For a computer backup record, scan the receipts, and keep them in a computer file with your worksheet.

ESTATE EXPENSES

Type of Expense	Date Incurred	Name of Payee	Description Purpose Of Expense	Amount	Date Paid	Comment Notes
Court costs						
Property repairs & maintenance						
Appraisals						

Type of Expense	Date Incurred	Name of Payee	Description Purpose Of Expense	Amount	Date Paid	Comment Notes
Auctioneer						
Representative fees (if not waived)						
Accountant fees						
Attorney fees (if hired)						
Postage						
Newspaper advertisements for notices						
Estate notice						
Creditor notice						
Other						

If the Estate Lacks Sufficient Funds

If the estate lacks sufficient cash to pay claims but has other assets, the next step is to examine property to be liquidated. Sale of property is within the personal representative's appointed powers, but it might be necessary to obtain permission from the court to sell assets. The will should specify instructions to the personal representative as to how to satisfy debts that are not covered by ready cash in the estate. If the will does not satisfactorily resolve this for you, it is wise to consult the beneficiaries to avoid, if possible, controversy over which property is selected for liquidation. This is one of the many estate matters that benefit from frank communication between you and the beneficiaries. If an agreement it is not reached in this way, state law will specify the order in which bequests in the will should be used to satisfy debts. Obligations will be paid on a partial, pro rata, basis, in an order of priority set by state law.

Protecting property from the expense and time delay of the probate process and from being exposed to diversion for payment of probate debt are high in the reasons why people like to use other methods of property transfer in their estate planning. The trust is a long-used method used to confer property and income on beneficiaries to avoid the probate process and mitigate tax obligations. A trust, though, can come into play in the probate estate, such as where a trust is created by the will or an existing freestanding trust is named as a beneficiary of the will. *The next chapter will explain all about trusts and how they enter into the estate-management process.*

CASE STUDY: A LOVED ONE'S EXPERIENCE

Lisa Capozzi
Los Angeles, California

Lisa Capozzi had never really had any experience with wills and estate planning until her father passed away. At 88 years old, he was in fairly good health, and his death was unexpected. Luckily, he had planned accordingly with an estate plan; unluckily, his family did not handle it well, and even today, problems still plague the family with the estate still up in the air.

"Five months ago my dad passed away unexpectedly," she said at the time of the interview. "He was still fairly active, driving his own car and traveling quite extensively. My six siblings and I knew he had some sort of written will, but we didn't really know how he had divided his assets.

The difficult part of this process after his passing is that, for one, things seem to be moving at a snail's pace. Not only that, there is a huge communication gap between the beneficiaries — myself and my siblings — and the executors — my dad's accountant, a brother-in-law, and my dad's second wife. No one is informing us what is supposed to happen or what is happening."

Capozzi said this lack of communication was maddening, creating a feeling of suspicion that either the money was being extorted or that fees for services and commissions on IRAs were mounting.

"This is very difficult, as we know the money my dad left for us is him and my mom's life's work," Capozzi added. "We're certain they would want us, not others, to benefit from all of their hard work."

Capozzi said her father did not talk much about money while he was alive, always being a bit secretive about his finances and keeping her mom in the dark as well. "In his death, in a way, he continued his secretive ways regarding money," Capozzi said.

Capozzi talked to countless attorneys and performed an extensive amount of research on the Internet, but there still did not seem to be any answers. This is just one example of how important it is to have your will or trust planned and understood by those among the living.

"There is extensive information about wills and trusts on the Internet and thousands of attorneys to contact, and yet, I still don't know how to protect the assets my dad set aside for us," she explained. "I've finally seen a copy of the will and trust. Yet, how would I know for certain that it is being executed properly? I don't have a law or accounting degree. I don't have money to hire an attorney to look after my interests. I'm frustrated during this very sad time in my life when I have now lost both my parents. I know the money can't bring them back, but it would certainly help to ease the financial difficulties my husband and I are plagued with during these volatile economic times."

Capozzi hopes a situation like this never happens to anyone else. "To anyone who has a will, share specifically what you have and what you are leaving to whom before you pass on," she advised. "It's pretty difficult to read your mind after you've died. If communication with your loved ones about your will is not possible, then at least leave specific directions for your accountant and/or attorney about the timeframe and methods for the execution of your will. The extra step will avoid frustration and stress for your loved ones."

Chapter 7

Trusts

The image many people have of a trust fund is a pot of money to support a child through college or an adult to live a carefree life without money concerns. But although trusts are handy devices to conserve wealth, you do not need to be independently rich to set up a trust. Trusts are significantly more diverse than the commonly accepted stereotype, and they can come into play in various ways when settling an estate.

There are many types of trusts with combinations of legal and tax implications, so there is no such thing as a "standard" trust. A book like this one can help you learn what a trust is, but beware of any "one-size-fits-all" trust explanation. For purposes of this book, the primary point to understand is that you can become involved with a trust in your capacity as the personal representative of an estate in two ways. One is when a trust was in place during the decedent's lifetime (an inter vivos trust), and the trust is a beneficiary of the will (referred to as a pour-over trust, because assets from the estate "pour over" from the estate into the trust). The other is when the will provisions create a new trust (a *testamentary* trust) with assets that already are a part of the probate estate.

Where trusts are concerned, especially if you are tasked with setting up a trust under the will, advice of legal counsel is advisable to ensure legal and tax implications are covered.

However, the steps to set up a trust and the elements of a trust are easy enough to understand: Identify the property to be included (the res), who benefits from the trust (beneficiary), who manages the trust (trustee), tax implications for all the people involved, and how the law governs all that activity.

Definition of a Trust

A trust is a legal arrangement that involves the transfer of property (trust res) from the original owner (grantor or trustor) to a person or a company for the purpose of holding and maintaining the property (trustee) until it is handed over to the beneficiary — the individual or institution designated to receive the property.

This is a simple enough definition, until you become entangled in various legal terms, laws, and taxes that relate to creation and management of a trust. There are also interchangeable terms, some of which are as confusing as the Greek or Roman terms from which they originate, a list of who is who and what is what is helpful. The following situation will assist you with recognizing the roles each person plays in a trust.

People: Uncle Mike wants to ensure his nephew, Bob, will have a place to set up a veterinary clinic after he finishes his education; Uncle Mike decides his house will be perfect. But Uncle Mike does not know when Bob will graduate, so he wants his grandson Charles to take care of the place and hold it in trust for Bob's benefit if he — Uncle Mike — dies before Bob is ready and able to launch his practice. If something happens to Charles, his wife, Kim, will then take on that responsibility. Because Uncle Mike is putting this in place during his lifetime, this is an inter vivos trust arrangement.

- **Trustor** (Uncle Mike): The person who sets up the trust. Other names commonly used are creator, donor, settlor, or grantor.

- **Beneficiary** (nephew Bob): The individual(s) or group(s) who will receive the income and/or property in the trust. This can be a single person, a group of people, one group, several groups, or a combination of any of these and might be institutions or charities.

- **Trustee** (grandson Charles): The person or company that will oversee or manage the trust once it is established. This person (or group) will make sure the property in the trust is safe and in good order until it is turned over to the beneficiary. This includes paying any taxes, performing repairs, or anything else an owner would do. The trustee acts as a fiduciary that is obligated to carry out the terms of the trust and can be paid for this effort, if terms for this are included in the trust language. In the case of Uncle Mike's house, Uncle Mike likely also would place cash in the trust designated for taking care of the house and to help Bob set up his veterinary practice. Charles would have the option of renting the house, if the trust does not limit his powers in this regard, as a source of income for the trust until Bob is ready to take possession. Institutions, such as a bank, also can be named as a trustee.

- **Successor trustee** (Kim, Charles' wife): Someone who will step in if the primary trustee is unable to serve or cannot continue to manage the trust. This person will have the same legal obligations for managing the trust as the original trustee.

The individual or company designated to serve as trustee carries a significant amount of responsibility and needs to be someone the grantor trusts implicitly (hence, the name "trust" for the legal agreement). Just like an estate personal representative, a trustee has a fiduciary responsibility to the trust and its beneficiary. The potential for a conflict of interest or being swayed by the temptation to do something inappropriate — such as stealing from the trust or neglecting the work required to oversee it — needs to be considered in selecting a trustee. Putting language in the trust documents that spells out the responsibilities of the trustee is essential, and creating a mechanism of oversight and removal will prevent beneficiaries from losing what is supposed to be theirs.

Trusts are substitutes for disposing of assets that would otherwise go through probate. Uncle Mike's house is an example. He puts his house into a trust during his lifetime. He can be the trustee if he chooses, until he dies, and then Charles could become the successor trustee, followed by Kim. Or, Uncle Mike can set up the trust where Charles is the trustee and Uncle Mike is a designated co-beneficiary with Bob during his lifetime, with the trust continuing for the sole benefit of Bob after Uncle Mike's death until Bob satisfies the conditions of the trust, i.e., completes his education and is licensed to open a veterinary practice.

Things and strings: Uncle Mike's house originally was part of 16 acres, but it now sits on four acres of land with an outbuilding to store the lawn tractor and other equipment. Several years ago, Uncle Mike sold off the other 12 acres and invested the money into a mutual fund. Uncle Mike had his lawyer set up a trust for the mutual fund and house together that gives Bob the interest from the mutual fund to pay tuition when it is due each school term, but the mutual fund principal will not go to Bob until he graduates from veterinary school. The house and property, also in Charles' care as trustee, will go to Bob after he graduates but only if he passes his veterinary board. If Bob does not pass his veterinary board within two years after graduation, then the house will go to Charles instead. If Bob graduates from veterinary school, he will receive the money in the trust. If he does not graduate from veterinary school by the time he is 30 years old, then the money and house will go to Charles.

- **Property:** Tangible and intangible items or assets that you own; when it draws interest, also referred to as principal. There are all kinds of legal terms for the "stuff" people own, so make sure the right words are used to identify everything from money in a safe or checking account to a rocking chair or commemorative baseball. This can be real property or real estate (such as a ten-acre farm), tangible personal property (the things you can touch, such as a lawn tractor and other equipment, jewelry, coin collection), or intangible personal property (financial assets such as certificates of deposit, intellectual property like a patent on an invention).

- **Trust agreement:** The legal document that spells out the terms of a trust, including the people involved in their various roles, and the conditions and the rules that must be followed

- **Funding a trust:** The placement of property (the res) in a trust; that same property will be called trust principal once it is under control of the trust agreement.

- **Trust provisions:** The clauses that spell out how you want your wishes carried out. Distribution provisions will identify to whom the income will be given and the frequency of those distributions (e.g., pay tuition when it is due). Special provisions encompass all requirements that are unique to the beneficiary or the assets (e.g., nephew graduates from college).

- **Legal title:** This gives the trustee ownership of the property in the trust for the duration of the trustee's responsibility (such as Uncle Mike's house in Charles' care; the trustee owns the house on behalf of the trust).

- **Beneficial title:** Also known as equitable title, this is the right of the person or institution designated as the beneficiary of the trust to take possession of or benefit from the property in the trust (e.g., Uncle Mike's house goes to Bob when Bob graduates and gets his veterinarian's license).

The plan can be incredibly clear, but whether the result matches that plan depends on the kind of trust constructed, the way the documents are worded, and the way the people involved carry out their tasks. Being a trustee is more than just whipping out a checkbook and signing a few papers now and then.

Considerations

Key questions for a personal representative to note when dealing with a trust in an estate include:

- What are the estate tax consequences, if any, related to the trust? If the will provides for a testamentary trust, is there a contingency provided in case the beneficiary of the trust has died before the testator? *Testamentary trusts will be explained in the next section.*

- What happens if the terms of a trust are not met — i.e., Bob quits veterinary school without finishing?

- If the will makes a bequest to an inter vivos trust, what happens if that trust no longer exists? What if the testator named a trustee for a testamentary trust and the named person died before the testator?

Facts that could affect the legality and terms of a trust include:

- Foreign-born spouse
- Non-biological "family" members

- Same-sex couples who are not married, or who are married in a state that does not recognize their marriage
- Living together — as opposed to a formal or common-law marriage, or in a state that does not recognize common-law marriage
- Adoption
- Frozen embryos of a married couple
- Pets
- Community marital property
- Divorce
- Multiple marriages — offspring and spouses
- Incapacitation
- Medical condition/serious illness
- Permanent disability
- Natural disaster affecting property
- Stock/real estate market crash

Again, always seek legal council immediately if you are faced with any trust issues you do not know how to resolve yourself.

Types of Trusts

A trust can be set up to take effect while the person is alive (inter vivos), or it can take effect after he or she dies (testamentary). Some can be changed (revocable), and some cannot be changed no matter what (irrevocable). Some trusts can be terminated or ended, while others cannot. A trust can result in a tax exemption or higher tax rate, depending on what the current tax law allows.

Some of the reasons for setting up a trust are tax benefits, avoiding probate, protecting assets from creditors, or making sure money is available "just in case" for things like education, severe illness, or a disability. Considering all life's possibilities, to decide which trust(s) would be helpful or the most appropriate in a given situation, is a daunting task. Another way to look at the situation is to consider the kinds of trusts that already exist and have defined legal and tax consequences.

Trusts fall into a number of categories that can be described by different criteria. One criterion is the beneficiary. A marital dedication trust is specific to the surviving, legal spouse of the deceased. A bypass trust will transfer property to someone other than your spouse, such as a child or grandchild, but allows the spouse to still benefit from the property in the trust. Many states even allow you to create a trust for your pets.

Another criterion is the reason for the trust. If you want to protect the beneficiary's property so that it is available for a specific reason when it is needed, the decedent could have used a protective or discretionary trust. A discretionary trust gives the trustee the ability to distribute income and property to a variety of beneficiaries; the trustor also has the option to control the distributions to a single beneficiary as the trustor deems is appropriate. Such an approach offers some flexibility, as does a dynasty trust (also known as a wealth trust); it can last for several generations or be set up to never end. This kind of trust helps people with a vast amount of wealth control the distribution of that money and property over a long period. However, many states limit non-charitable trusts to 90 years.

The overarching requirements of a trust create another group. A split-interest trust means more than one individual benefits from the trust: One person or charity would have an interest in the trust for a specific period, and then another person or charity receives the property that remains.

A support trust requires a trustee to pay only the income and property necessary to cover the cost of education or assistance, such as health care or nursing home fees, of the beneficiaries.

Some trusts are automatically irrevocable. However, many trusts can be set up as revocable or irrevocable, with a variety of conditions that put the trust into one of the categories already defined by tax law. These laws continue changing to keep up with the creative efforts to avoid taxes.

The following are the various types of trusts that might arise in the context of an estate:

- **Burial trust:** This trust provides the funds necessary to cover the cost of burial or cremation arrangements. This can be a revocable trust during a person's lifetime, but after death, it becomes irrevocable, and the trust cannot be used for anything else.

- **Charitable trust:** A charitable trust provides the benefit of tax-free gifts for the donor. A charitable remainder trust gives gifts of interest income that are paid to specific beneficiaries such as a spouse for a specific period; at the end of that period, a charity receives whatever is left in the trust. A charitable lead trust, or a front trust, gives the charity a specific gift before all other beneficiaries receive anything. These are both split-interest trusts. Split-interest trusts make distributions to both charitable and non-charitable beneficiaries, while providing tax benefits to their donor.

- **Crummey trust:** The Crummey trust is an exceedingly complicated trust normally set up in conjunction with an irrevocable life insurance trust to make the payments for a life insurance policy. Like most trusts, this kind of trust requires an estate-planning attorney.

- **Educational trust:** This protective trust sets aside money specifically for education-related expenses, such as tuition or training fees, books, or supplies. These trusts regularly include provisions to stop payments if the student drops out of school or flunks many classes.

- **Generation-skipping transfer trust (GSTT):** The GSTT is a form of tax-saving trust designed to benefit multiple generations after the trustor dies.

- **Grantor-retained trusts:** These are irrevocable and non-charitable trusts, which means they cannot be changed and the beneficiary is not a charity. There are three common types: A Grantor-Retained Annuity Trust (GRAT) gives a fixed amount of money at predetermined times, often at regularly scheduled intervals; a Grantor-Retained Unit Trust (GRUT) pays a specific percentage to the beneficiary; and a Grantor-Retained Incomes Trust (GRIT) designates specific people to receive certain property, such as stocks or a house, but the income or use of the property stays with you until your death.

- **Living trust:** Created while the trustor is still alive, this trust allows the trustor to be the grantor, trustee, and beneficiary if he or she so chooses.

- **Marital dedication trust:** Puts property into a trust that is exclusively for the decedent's spouse, who decides what happens to the property after his or her death.

- **Minor trust:** A trust set to benefit a minor is a way to give gifts to minors that avoids the gift tax and keeps the property safe until the minor becomes an adult and can take ownership of the trust of the property.

- **QTIP:** A Qualified Terminable Interest Property trust is a marital deduction trust, but instead of the surviving spouse deciding who gets the property after the trustor's death, the trustor makes the decision by setting up the trust.

- **Spendthrift trust:** This trust is set up for someone who the trustor believes will not be able to handle money well, i.e., someone who is mentally incompetent or might have financial problems and needs protection from creditors. The beneficiary does not own the property in the trust, just the payments that are made from the trust. The beneficiary's creditors cannot reach the trust property.

- **Special needs trust:** This is a support trust for a disabled person under the age of 65 (trustor or another person). The trust makes payments on the beneficiary's behalf, as required by the state, as reimbursement. After the beneficiary dies, the property in the trust is paid to other beneficiaries. This trust is designed to protect the trust property from seizure by the government or a creditor.

- **Supplemental needs trust:** This is a support trust designed to provide income to an elderly or disabled person to supplement his or her income, but it is structured in a way that does not reduce or jeopardize the eligibility of that person to receive public or private benefits. This trust is designed to protect the trust property from seizure by the government or a creditor.

- **Testamentary trust:** Created by the terms of the will, as previously mentioned. This type of trust does not come into effect until the trustor dies and the trust property is created with probate assets. This is most likely the trust you will see if you are handling an estate.

- **Totten trust:** This is a bank account that, upon the trustor's death, immediately passes to the named beneficiary. The account funds are not subject to probate.

There are also special trusts for specific types of property such as real estate, life insurance, or pension benefits. To set up a testamentary trust as instructed by the will in your estate, enlist the help of a lawyer who can make sure all the necessary steps are taken to ensure the trust will act exactly as specified by the decedent.

Minor children as beneficiaries

A trust could arise by operation of law when bequests in a will are designated to minor children. These will fall under the Uniform Transfer for Minors Act (UTMA). Most states have adopted this legislation, which provides for a custodian account to be set up for a minor with an adult named as custodian on the account until the minor reaches age 18.

A custodian account, which can be in the form of a trust, allows you to deposit money or property in an account set up by a bank or a brokerage firm. In the context of a bequest of money or other valuable property to a minor in a will, you as the executor will need to oversee the setting up of a custodial arrangement under UTMA, with the minor's parent as trustee or other person you deem appropriate, if the will is silent on this point. The probate court will want to know how gifts to minors are being protected for the minors under UTMA or specific rules of the probate court concerning gifts to minors. The trust arrangement for the minor will continue until the child reaches 18, 21, or 25, depending on the state law's age cap for this purpose.

Keep in mind the following for UTMA:

☑ Some states hand over the ownership of the account to the child when he or she turns 18, and the custodian has no say after that.

☑ Accounts for children over the age of 13 are subject to federal income tax at the children's tax rate for interest earned. This will be lower than the adult custodian's tax rate, but the requirement needs to be understood.

☑ Creating this kind of account is not a substitute for naming a legal guardian for children in a will, although that legal guardian also can be the custodian on a UTMA account.

Although trusts provide some excellent benefits, they are not the perfect solution for everything. One benefit is that some trusts can reduce the amount of taxes that have to be paid before and after the decedent dies. But if the trust is not set up properly, it might have to pay income tax, including penalties, if it is determined belatedly that taxes are owed. A trust can protect assets from creditors of the trustor or the trust's beneficiaries, but, again, only if it is created properly.

A trust is more private than a will. The latter becomes public record upon death, in the probate court. The will's provisions will disclose the details of the estate to anyone who wants to review it. A trust is not a public document (unless it is created within the will).

CASE STUDY:
TAXES AND GIFTS:
THE MYSTERIES

Tax laws are not designed to protect estates. Instead, they are designed to collect as much as possible from estates in order to raise revenue for the federal and state governments. The estate laws of each state do provide some protection, but they are designed to put the rights of creditors first and your beneficiaries last. A competent estate-planning attorney can design an estate plan to minimize taxes and preserve as much of the estate as possible.

As technology has advanced, the process for estate planning has become easier and simpler. Estate planning professionals typically have an estate plan fully in place in just a few days or weeks. The client's time can be minimized to just a few hours.

One of the big mistakes that is seen in estate plans is to leave a single dollar to someone whom you do not want to leave anything. This is not the right way to do this. It may cost thousands of dollars for the administrator to hire an investigator to track down an estranged heir to deliver the single dollar. The best language is to name the person being left out and state that they are intentionally omitted. Stating the reason could lead to a successful challenge if it is not worded properly, so it is better not to state the reason. Disinherited persons may wish to contest not being included, but they must prove that you were incompetent or unaware of your family, your environment, or your estate or that there was fraud, mistake, or undue influence at the time you signed the estate plan. Without one or more of these elements, they have no hope of winning.

For gifts, the right choice to go with is dependent on what the client wants to see happen. It's advised to tell clients that they do not know how much money they will need to live on for the rest of their lives. If they start giving it away before they die, it may not be available in a time of need. Gifting is typically only best for the very wealthy who know that their financial needs will be met no matter what happens.

There is plenty of hope if planning takes place before your incapacity. You can handpick who will take over, without the interference of any outsider. If no plan is in place at the time of your incapacity, you may find yourself at the discretion of the probate court and a court-appointed guardian (who also may be a probate attorney), which could cost your estate tens of thousands of dollars per year.

Surviving Spouse, Minor Children, and Other Beneficiaries of the Estate

In many states, there are protective provisions in the probate process for a surviving spouse and minor children of a decedent. States that have a homestead exemption, for example, provide an opportunity to keep surviving spouse and minor children in their home, at least for some period. Most states have a statute facilitating a quick and easy transfer of decedent's car to his or her surviving spouse. Spousal protection laws step in to provide a surviving spouse a statutory portion of the estate if the decedent cut the spouse out of the will.

The purpose of laws like these is to provide a measure of continuity and stability in a family that is aggrieved by the loss of a spouse and/or parent.

Rights of Surviving Spouse and Minor Children

In most cases, the surviving spouse will be the primary, if not the sole, beneficiary of the will. Many marital partners create reciprocal wills in which each names the other as sole beneficiary. This is often the case even when children are in the family because the spouses view the children as becoming eligible for inheritance only after the remaining spouse dies. In the case of young children, the remaining spouse will need the resources to care for the children on his or her own.

Sometimes the surviving spouse is not named in the will. This could happen because the will predates the marriage and was never updated by the deceased spouse. It also could happen because the decedent intentionally omitted his or her spouse. In most states, if one spouse cuts the surviving spouse out of the will, the law provides the surviving spouse the right to claim a portion of the estate, regardless of the testator's personal feelings about it. A procedure in the probate court for the spouse is called "taking against the will." This spousal right comes ahead of any bequests to others the testator made in the will. (Note this only applies to existing spouses, not ex-spouses, future spouses who are only engaged, or unmarried partners.)

When the personal representative opens the estate and receives letters of authority to proceed, he or she provides a copy of the will and notice of rights to the surviving spouse. The surviving spouse needs to be advised of the options provided by statute as to the right to elect to demand his or her statutory share of the estate. Forms are to be filed regarding this situation. This is one set of circumstances where having the advice of legal counsel is advisable for the personal representative of the estate.

The size of the spouse's statutory portion will depend on whether there are also surviving children of the deceased. If there is a surviving spouse with no children, then the spousal share will be greater. For example, in Ohio, the spousal share with no surviving children is 50 percent of the estate. If two or more children of the decedent also are surviving, then the spousal share is one-third of the estate. The statutory spousal share only applies to people who are married at the time of death, not ex-spouses.

The surviving spouse also is the first in line to inherit as next of kin in the intestate estate. If there is a surviving spouse with no children of the decedent, the surviving spouse inherits the entire estate. If there are children of the decedent surviving, then the intestate estate will be divided between the spouse and child(ren) according to the provisions of the state's statute of descent and distribution.

Unlike the surviving spouse, minor children can be purposefully omitted from a will. Because the probate process can drag on, all states provide some sort of protection for a surviving spouse and in some cases, minor children of the decedent, under a concept called "homestead rights." A homestead law permits the surviving spouse and minor children of the decedent to remain in the decedent's home for some time even if the home ultimately will go to someone else under the terms of the will. Some states even give the surviving spouse the option of living in the home for the rest of his or her life.

A surviving spouse also might be able to apply for a "family allowance" from the probate estate during the tendency of its administration for the support of the spouse and minor children. The family allowance has top priority over the other debts of the estate and must be paid even if such payment would completely deplete the estate of its assets. This means that creditors might go unpaid and bequests in a will might not go to their respective recipients, in order to satisfy the family allowance. The court determines the amount of the family allowance. The personal representative for the estate, as well as beneficiaries and even creditors, might disagree with the amount claimed by the surviving spouse. The court will consider everyone's position and such factors as the size of the estate, the spouse's age and health, the standard of living at the time of decedent's death, and the number of minor children.

When a surviving spouse is the parent of the decedent's minor children, there is no issue of guardianship for the children within the probate of the estate. A minor child orphaned by the death of the decedent is a different question entirely. Often, a parent nominates a guardian or parent guardians in his or her will to cover this potential circumstance.

CASE STUDY:
THE DISINHERITED SPOUSE

(Fictitious names used for privacy)

Philip and Harriett, residents of Ohio, were legally married in 1940. During their marriage, they had three children. In 1955, Philip moved to a neighboring city and took up residence with his unmarried sister in a large home in his sister's name. Philip and Harriet never divorced. Philip would visit the children periodically at his former home with Harriet and continued to pay Harriet's household bills and the children's needs. The children grew up, went to college, and moved into their own homes. Harriet went back to school herself and got a professional job. Philip paid her tuition.

At the age of 80, Philip died. Harriet was then 70. Until that time Philip had continued to pay monthly support to Harriet. They never divorced or made their separation official. They lived apart under their own arrangement as dictated by Philip.

Philip's will left everything he owned to his sister. He left nothing to Harriet or to any of his grown children. He appointed his sister to be the executrix of the will. He stated that he had paid Harriet throughout their lifetime, including her education into a new profession and saw no need to include her in the will.

Philip's idea about this did not matter under Ohio probate law. At the time of his death, Philip had a surviving spouse: Harriet. Harriet is entitled by law to a portion of Philip's estate. Ohio law states that where there is a surviving spouse and children of the deceased, the spouse is entitled to one-third of the estate. Philip's sister, as the executrix must notify Harriet of her rights to her portion of the estate under Ohio law and give Harriet a copy of the will. Harriet has the option of (1) waiving her right to anything from the estate, or (2) taking against the will, that is, asserting her claim to her statutory portion of Philip's estate. In this case, Harriet took against the will. The estate was worth $750,000, most of it in cash and investments. Harriet was entitled to $250,000, and the balance to Philip's sister (after satisfaction of any debts and taxes owed). The children had no legal claim against the will.

Guardianship

Whether for a child or a disabled adult, appointing a guardian of another person is a legal action. A child's godparents do not automatically become guardians upon a parent's death, despite cultural beliefs and patterns. The court is ultimately responsible for appointing a guardian for the minor children. The court is not bound by the decedent's provision in the will but certainly will give it serious consideration. The estate's personal representative represents the wishes of the testator in this regard, although other considerations could come into play, such as the nominated guardian refusing the appointment or not being competent or available to assume the role.

The person whom the testator nominates to be a guardian is not required to accept the appointment, either. If he or she does, it is the would-be guardian's responsibility to petition the court for appointment as guardian. Your role as personal representative will be to contact the person named in the will about the decedent's wishes. As with some of the other complications that can arise in probate, this situation might benefit from advice of legal counsel.

It might be helpful to you in your role as personal representative to have an understanding of the expectations and demands upon the guardian for a minor appointed in this situation. The guardian for a minor will be responsible for things such as food, clothing, and shelter. However, he or she also will be responsible for managing assets in the child's name and providing for things such as education and health care. Compatibility of lifestyle, culture, and family dynamics also should be considered. The court's mandate is to consider what is in the best interest of the child. The same can be true for the guardian of an adult, who is responsible for paying bills on behalf of the person and making sure his or her place of residence is appropriate, clean, and safe. The estate's personal representative is in the position of assessing what would best satisfy the intent and wishes of the deceased were he or she able to speak and to advocate that position to the court. Also, a guardian can be named solely to look after property for a minor or disabled adult. A property guardian or property manager is a legal adult who takes responsibility for the oversight of property inherited by a minor. Children under the age of 18 can inherit property, but they are only allowed to own that property legally with adult supervision; an adult must have the responsibility of managing it. Just because a 17-year-old can inherit a car does not mean he or she is "in charge."

Such advocacy can become necessary when family members contest a testator's appointment in the will. A guardianship hearing could be necessary if family members are unhappy with the testator's choice. As the estate representative, you represent the testator's voice, if you have any knowledge at all to contribute about the testator's decision. The court will appoint a guardian ad litem for the minor for purposes of the controversy in the court. This person, usually a lawyer, independently represents the child's interests at the cost of the estate until the guardianship question is resolved. Fortunately, the ultimate appointment of the guardian is the court's responsibility, not yours.

Guardianship appointment by will is an intensely personal decision made by the testator. When you are the personal representative of an intestate estate, you do not have the benefit of the decedent's final wishes expressed in a will. In this situation, the court will look to the nearest relatives first as potential guardians.

Chapter 9

Taxes

axes are one of the many necessary considerations in managing an estate. Two categories of taxes might be involved. One is the filing of the decedent's final income tax returns (federal, state, and local). The other is the assessment and payment of estate-related taxes: estate, inheritance, and gift taxes. Taxes are estate debts and take priority over most other creditor claims.

Income Tax

The final federal income tax for decedent is filed on Form 1040 (or a version thereof). The deadline is April 15 in the year following the year of decedent's death. This is an obligation of the estate's personal representative. If no estate is filed, it is an obligation of the next of kin.

The estate itself will be subject to income tax (filed separately, Form 1041) if the estate receives income of $600 or more. Such income can derive from rental property and interest on investments, for example.

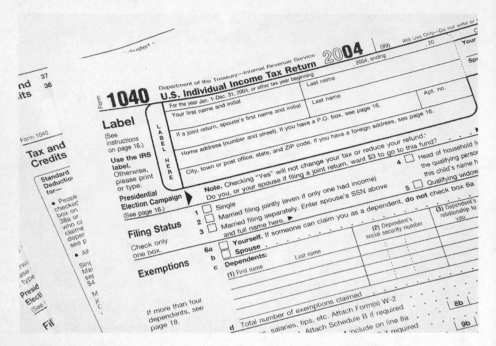

Estate Tax

Estate tax can be imposed by two possible sources: federal government and decedent's state of primary residence, where the estate is being probated.

Estate tax requirements have been fluctuating with changes of the laws in recent years. Under the statute enacted by Congress in December 2010, the minimum net estate value to subject to federal estate tax is $5 million for 2011 and $5.12 million for 2012 at a tax rate of 35 percent. Estates under these net valuations are exempt from federal taxes. This law is set to expire on December 31, 2012. Unless Congress enacts a new law, the estate tax will revert to a lower exemption of $1 million with a tax rate of 55 percent. The following summarizes the federal estate tax as it stands for the years 2009 to 2013:

Year	Tax exemption limit (Estates up to this amount are not taxed.)	Highest tax rate to be levied
2009	$3.5 million	45%
2010	No tax	
2011	$5 million	35%
2012	$5.12 million	35%
2013	$1 million	55%

State levies of estate tax are also in flux, as many states have historically tied their estate tax approach to what is going on in the federal arena. Others are delinked from the federal plan or do not levy an estate tax. When the federal government abolished estate tax for 2010, many states did as well. Then, the subsequent federal law at the end of 2010 reinstated federal estate tax. Following that, some states hastily returned to estate tax. For example, Delaware has reinstated its estate tax for deaths occurring July 1, 2009, through July 1, 2013. Hawaii, which had no estate tax, instituted it beginning May 1, 2010 (for estates of $3,600,000 and over). Oklahoma and Kansas, which had estate taxes in 2009, have since had no estate tax. On the other hand, Ohio had its own estate tax, unrelated to the federal scheme, applicable to estates valued at $338,333; however, by a law enacted June 30, 2011, Ohio has abolished its estate tax beginning with deaths occurring on and after January 1, 2013.

Clearly, the only way to be sure about applicable federal and estate taxes is to check what is in place for the date of death and year of your specific estate. Determine if estate tax applies for each, according to your estate's valuation. If it is a large estate, consider the services of a CPA or attorney for tax assistance. *A chart of the current estate and inheritance tax status by state is included in Appendix A of this book.* Because this area of law continues to be in flux, use this chart as a guide and double-check the status of your particular state.

Property included in estate tax calculation

In determining the estate's value for estate tax purposes, all assets in which the decedent had an interest at the time of death are included, not just the probate assets. The valuation of the gross estate might be lowered by certain deductions. One significant deduction is the marital deduction, which allows the subtraction of all property that passes from the decedent to the surviving spouse. Other allowable deductions include funeral expenses, costs of administration of the estate, paid claims against the estate, unpaid mortgages, and charitable bequests. As with the application of the estate tax itself, allowable deductions must be checked with the current law. The reduction of the gross value by the allowable deductions provides the net valuation for tax purpose. *The current federal estate tax form, IRS Form 706, is included in this book's Appendix D.* This form's updates, including its instructions, are available online at **irs.gov**.

Inheritance Tax

Another tax relating to estates is state inheritance tax. This tax is levied on the distribution of assets from the estate to the estate beneficiaries, rather than the estate value itself. States that currently levy inheritance tax are District of Columbia, Indiana, Iowa, Kentucky, Maryland, Nebraska, New Jersey, and Pennsylvania. These states exempt surviving spouses from inheritance tax, however, and all except Nebraska and Pennsylvania exempt the decedent's blood descendants. All others, friends for example, who receive bequests are subject to the tax because they are not exempt from it. Life insurance proceeds are not included in the calculation of inheritance tax. The inheritance tax filing deadline varies among these states, but generally, the time limit ranges from nine to 18 months after the date of decedent's death.

Maryland and New Jersey at present are the only two states that collect both estate tax and inheritance tax.

Gift Tax

Gift taxes often are overlooked. The personal representative should review whether gift tax applies to the estate. Currently, gifts up to a maximum of $13,000 per year per individual recipient are exempt from imposition of federal gift tax. Also, federal law allows deferral of the gift tax for a lifetime exemption of (currently) $5.12 million. In this case, the gift amount is combined with the estate tax minimum exemption (currently $5.12 million). However, if the personal representative finds that the decedent made gifts of $5.12 million before death, those gifts are added to the estate value and will be taxed to the extent the combined net value exceeds $5.12 million (or other exemption amount, depending on the law's requirement at the time). The purpose behind this is readily apparent. A decedent will not avoid tax on the estate by giving away all or substantial amount of the assets in the year before death. To the extent the gifts exceed the allowable tax exemptions, they will be taxed unless no one individual received more than $13,000 or another deduction applies (e.g. charitable recipient). A separate exemption from all of this is gifts to a spouse, which enjoy an unlimited exemption.

CASE STUDY:
TAX ADVISORY FROM THE IRS
Internal Revenue Service (IRS)
800-829-1040
Hours of Operation: Monday - Friday,
7 a.m. - 10 p.m. your local time
(Alaska & Hawaii follow Pacific Time)
www.irs.gov

The IRS is the ultimate source for all things related to taxation. Its website offers extensive resources for those who wish to learn more about anything related to taxes. What follows is a copy of the frequently asked questions (FAQ) on the Estate Taxes page. The IRS is not in the habit of helping people figure out how to reduce their tax bills, but they will give you all you need to know to be "legal." Simply achieving the goal of compliance with tax law is not something even the FAQ can guarantee. The recurring qualifiers and other sources you need to check make it clear that dealing with estate taxes on your own is risky.

When can I expect the Estate Tax Closing Letter?
There can be some variation, but for returns that are accepted as filed and contain no other errors or special circumstances, expect to wait about four to six months after the return is filed to receive your closing letter. Returns selected for examination or reviewed for statistical purposes will take longer.

What is included in the estate?
The gross estate of the decedent consists of an accounting of everything you own or have certain interests in at the date of death. The fair market value of these items is used, not necessarily what was paid for them or what their values were when acquired. The total of all of these items is the gross estate. The includible property may consist of cash and securities, real estate, insurance, trusts, annuities, business interests, and other assets. Keep in mind that the gross estate likely will include non-probate as well as probate property.

The decedent owns a one-half interest in a farm (or building or business) with his/her brother (sister, friend, other). What is included?
Depending on how the **one-half** interest is held and treated under state

law — and how it was acquired — you probably only would include **one-half** of its value in the gross estate. However, many other factors influence this answer, so visit with a tax or legal professional to make that determination.

What is excluded from the estate?

The gross estate does not include property owned solely by the decedent's spouse or other individuals. Lifetime gifts that are complete (no powers or other control over the gifts are retained) are not included in the gross estate (but taxable gifts are used in the computation of the estate tax). Life estates given to the decedent by others in which the decedent has no further control or power at the date of death are not included.

What deductions are available to reduce the estate tax?

1. Marital deduction: One of the primary deductions for married decedents is the marital deduction. All property included in the gross estate that passes to the surviving spouse is eligible for the marital deduction. The property must pass "outright." In some cases, certain life estates also qualify for the marital deduction.
2. Charitable deduction: If the decedent leaves property to a qualifying charity, it is deductible from the gross estate.
3. Mortgages and debt
4. Administration expenses of the estate
5. Losses during estate administration

What other information do I need to include with the return?

Among other items listed:

1. Copies of the death certificate
2. Copies of the decedent's will and/or relevant trusts
3. Copies of appraisals
4. Copies of relevant documents regarding litigation involving the estate
5. Documentation of any unusual items shown on the return (partially included assets, losses, near-date-of-death transfers, others)

What is "fair market value?"

Fair market value is defined as "the price at which the property would change hands between a willing buyer and a willing seller, neither being under any compulsion to buy or to sell, and both having reasonable knowledge of relevant facts. The fair market value of a particular item of property includible in the decedent's gross estate is not to be determined by a forced sale price. Nor is the fair market value of an item of property to be determined by the sale price of the item in a market other than that in which such item is most commonly sold to the public, taking into account the location of the item wherever appropriate."

What about the value of my family business/farm?
The fair market values of interests owned by the decedent are includible in the gross estate at date of death. However, for certain farms or businesses operated as a family farm or business, reductions to these amounts may be available.

In the case of a qualifying family farm, IRC §2032A allows a reduction from value of up to $820,000.

If the decedent owned an interest in a qualifying family-owned business, a deduction from the gross estate of up to $1,100,000 may be available under IRC §2057.

What if I do not have everything ready for filing by the due date?
The estate's representative may request an extension of time to file for up to six months from the due date of the return. However, the correct amount of tax is still due by the due date, and interest is accrued on any amount still owed by the due date that is not paid at that time.

Whom should I hire to represent me and prepare and file the return?
The IRS cannot make recommendations about specific individuals, but there are several factors to consider:
1. How complex is the estate? By the time most estates reach $1 million, there is usually some complexity involved, even if federal taxes are not triggered.
2. How large is the estate?
3. In what condition are the decedent's records?
4. How many beneficiaries are there, and are they cooperative?
5. Do I need an attorney, CPA, enrolled agent (EA), or other professional(s)?

With these questions in mind, it is a good idea to discuss the matter with several attorneys and CPAs or EAs. Ask about how much experience they have had, and ask for referrals. This process should be similar to locating a good physician. Locate other individuals that have had similar experiences and ask for recommendations. Finally, after the individual(s) are employed and begin to work on estate matters, make sure the lines of communication remain open so that there are no surprises during administration or if the estate tax return is examined.

Finally, most estates engage the services of both attorneys and CPAs or EAs. The attorney usually handles probate matters and reviews the impact of documents on the estate tax return. The CPA or EA often handles the actual return preparation and some representation of the estate in matters with the IRS. However, some attorneys handle all the work. CPAs and EAs also may handle most of the work, but cannot take care of probate matters and other situations where a law license is required. In addition, other professionals (such as appraisers, surveyors, financial advisers, and others) may need to be engaged during this time.

Do I have to talk to the IRS during an examination?
You do not have to be present during an examination unless an IRS representative needs to ask specific questions. Although you may represent yourself during an examination, most executors prefer that professional(s) they have employed handle this phase of administration. They may delegate authority for this by signing a designation on the Form 706 itself or executing Form 2848, "Power of Attorney."

What if I disagree with the examination proposals?
You have many rights and avenues of appeal if you disagree with any proposals made by the IRS.

What happens if I sell property that I have inherited?
The sale of such property usually is considered the sale of a capital asset and might be subject to capital gains (or loss) treatment. However, IRC §1014 provides that the basis of property acquired from a decedent is its fair market value at the date of death, so there is usually little or no gain to account for if the sale occurs soon after the date of death. Remember, the rules are different for determining the basis of property received as a lifetime gift.

Chapter 10

Settling and Closing the Estate

Your primary initial tasks in administering the estate are to locate and inventory the estate assets. This includes identifying the assets that have been designated by the testator in the will for the testator's beneficiaries named in the will. Liquid assets — that is cash and money, stocks and bonds, and similar financial funds on deposit — are moved into estate accounts. *This was covered in Chapter 5. Refer back to it for more information.* Before assets can be distributed to beneficiaries of the estate, whether as stated in the will or under the statute of descent and distribution for an intestate estate, the debts of the estate must be determined and paid, including tax obligations, if any. *These debts were covered in Chapter 6.*

An exception to paying money out to a beneficiary before satisfying creditors is the homestead allowance discussed in Chapter 8, if it is available in your state to surviving spouse and minor children.

Managing the Estate Assets

Because assets are held for a time during the pendency of the estate, one of your responsibilities as you move toward settling the estate is to manage these assets in a manner that conserves their value and the value of the estate. This chapter will explain how to manage these assets and conclude with advice for distributing them to their appropriate beneficiaries.

Wasting assets

Some items do not hold their value as time passes. In addition, some of these items might also cost money to maintain. An example is livestock. It is recommended that livestock that is part of an estate be sold as quickly as possible for the highest price obtainable, thereby converting this type of asset to money that can be invested for the estate or used to pay creditors. Another example is equipment that must sit unused and housed and kept in working order as part of the estate. This type of asset depreciates daily and should be sold for the best price obtainable rather than keeping it is a burden on the estate. Vehicles also require storage, upkeep, and insurance to protect them and any liability associated with them, but at the same time, their market value continues to depreciate. The estate personal representative has the power to make the decision to sell an asset, particularly when he or she needs to liquidate tangible property to pay creditors, satisfy a specific cash bequest in the will, or divide the interest in the property among more than one entitled beneficiary.

However, if a "wasting" asset has been specifically itemized as an in-kind bequest in the will, or if the beneficiaries disagree on its sale, the representative must obtain agreement to the sale in writing from the beneficiaries (and also legal intestate heirs of any exist who are not named in the will). If the agreement is not possible for any reason, apply to the court for an order approving the sale in advance.

It is always best to have the estate beneficiaries and legal heirs (if they are not named in the will, or if the estate is intestate) agree to sales of assets out of the estate during its pendency, even when the power of the estate representative to do so is clear or the sale is necessary to satisfy the terms of the will or pay taxes or creditors. If a beneficiary or heir does not agree, he or she might file an objection with the court post-sale, which will be an unwanted, unnecessary, and costly complication in settling the estate. Also, some courts might require an order authorizing a sale as part of their procedures, so be sure to check your court's procedure in advance of transacting a sale.

Making investments for the estate

Because money assets of the estate are not paid out for obligations and distribution immediately, the estate representative should review short-term investment of funds. Investments only can be made in a manner authorized by the will, by state law, or as approved by court order. However, typical safe investments would include FDIC-protected interest-bearing accounts in the bank and short-term federal government bonds. Other types of investments that require payment of commissions to brokers or are considered risky are not recommended, unless specifically authorized in the will. On the other hand, you can make any investment that is approved in writing by all the beneficiaries or approved by court order.

Also, investments should not be tied up for times where penalties attach to early withdrawal from the account or fund. Although an estate sometimes can take a year or more to settle, funds are needed during that time and need to be available when payments are required on behalf of the estate and ultimate distribution to beneficiaries comes due. For this reason, the personal representative can liquidate stocks, bonds, and other such investments that are part of the estate immediately when the funds are needed to pay estate obligations. The one caution here would be regarding stock or bonds that are specifically identified in the will for a specific bequest (for example, "my 1000 shares of IBM to my daughter, Rose"). Those shares should not be liquidated if it is not necessary to do so, and it would be prudent to obtain the agreement of Rose or a court order authorizing the sale if it is necessary.

If the estate does not have a large amount of money considering what will be needed to pay creditors, or if the estate is sufficiently simple to be able to settle it expeditiously, then the investment decision is likely to encompass no more than an interest-bearing checking account, if this option is available at the bank, or an estate savings account linked to a checking account. In the fictitious estate of Jason Little in Chapter 3, Charlie Lightfoot had $60,000 in the estate. Considering that Jason had the likelihood of debts to settle plus the straightforward, uncomplicated nature of the estate, Charlie had no reason to consider an aggressive investment plan for this money.

Real estate

Real property that is an estate asset has to be maintained by the estate. This includes insurance, as was discussed in Chapter 5. This is an obligation of the personal representative, who can be held personally liable for failing to do so if as a result the property is damaged and loses value. This does not include making improvements to the property, however. Therefore, if anything breaks within the house, such as the plumbing, the estate can pay for its repair. However, the estate will not pay for the expansion of the house or adding another wing, for example. Remember that you will be held accountable to prove all the expenses paid by the estate are valid expenses.

You might choose to have someone stay in the house while the estate is being settled. Any expenses incurred by the house sitter within reason can be paid out of the estate's account. If the person to whom it is bequeathed by will or to whom it passes by intestate distribution already occupies the house, this is also fine. Bear in mind, though, that this person must understand that this interim residence is not an ownership situation, and that he or she is subject to the oversight of the estate's personal representative and ultimately the court, if necessary, until the property is transferred. If the estate's financial condition requires the property to be sold, then the beneficiary's residence could be only temporary. If multiple beneficiaries are disputing occupation of the property, the personal representative may need to make the decision to have a dispassionate third party caretaker of the property as an interim measure.

The estate representative can sell real property. The will might direct that it must be sold and the proceeds used in a specific way or divided among named beneficiaries. In this case, the will controls. Depending on the state, you might still need an order from the court authorizing the sale. The property must be appraised for a sale as well as for the estate inventory. The sale can be handled through listing the property with a Realtor, but bear in mind this means a commission must be paid, which must be factored into the sale. You also can choose to sell it out of the estate as a "sell by owner" arrangement, which removes the cost of a sales commission from the equation. *Sale of out of state property will involve an ancillary proceeding as discussed in Chapter 5.*

Personal property

Any asset that is not real estate is personal property. As personal representative, you must collect and inventory the decedent's personal property. Photographing the items, especially those subject to specific bequests or sale, is a good way to catalog the item's existence and its condition. This protects you as the representative responsible for it and provides documentation for the estate records.

Considerations of keeping personal property items for distribution versus sale depends on the will provisions, the need to sell items to cover debt and costs of the estate, and the "wasting" nature of the property, as described above. Communication with the estate's beneficiaries is often most important when it comes to items of the deceased's personal property, especially of sentimental value. Some of these items might not even have a monetary value in terms of sale. For example, who gets the family photo album kept by the decedent can be the center of a disagreement. One creative executrix had two perfect duplicates made of a family photo album (part of the residuary estate that the testator mother had designated to be divided among her three adult children) to settle a dispute among the three, at a cost to the estate of $50. No one disputed the cost and all three got the photo album.

Not all disputes can be settled easily and might require the court to resolve the matter. An alternative to a formal court hearing is mediation. In this approach, a neutral party skilled in resolving disagreements mediates among the parties. If the squabbling beneficiaries and/or heirs agree to pay a mediator to engage in this process, the ultimate cost to the estate will be much less than a contested court hearing that will involve lawyers and court costs.

Business property

If the decedent left an interest, sole or in part, in an active business as part of the estate assets, the business either will need to be continued and managed by someone, or closed and liquidated. Ideally, the decedent will have provided for what should happen as part of the business plan in the business-governing documents or in the will.

If other business owners or partners are involved, they might want to continue the business. If the will is silent on what the decedent intended, you will have to evaluate the situation in terms of what is in the best interest for the estate. That is where your obligation lies. This is a complication of the estate representation in which the advice of legal counsel, and most likely the advice of an accountant, is recommended and useful. The decision points will depend on the nature of the decedent's involvement

in the business and how his or her withdrawal from the business by death affects the rest of the estate. Whether the business remains active or is closed, there will be matters relating to its operation and closing that will involve the estate and possibly the probate court's involvement authorizing certain actions.

Distribution of Estate Assets to Beneficiaries

When all the estate costs of administration, debts, and taxes are paid, the remaining assets can be distributed to the beneficiaries designated in the will or to the legal heirs if the estate is intestate. With distribution, the estate can be closed.

Depending on the state and your local court's procedure, you first will need to file a fiduciary's account, often called a final accounting, with the court for approval. This accounting lists the assets of the estate, receipts of the estate (such as interest paid on investments or savings, income to decedent collected by the estate, etc.), itemizes all the payments made (with receipts attached), and the assets remaining. Notice of the final account goes to all beneficiaries and legal heirs because they have the right to review the accounting and dispute it if they have reason. When the court is satisfied and approves the final account, you are ready to distribute the remaining assets to the beneficiaries. Some courts might provide the option of combining this step, which might be possible for simple estates, as we did in the hypothetical case for the Estate of Jason Little in Chapter 3. Usually, it is best to have the court approve the final accounting first to be assured there are no issues before disposing of the remaining assets in the estate. Being methodical takes more time but travels a smoother road.

Distribution is made according to the will, or if no will, under the state law for intestate distribution. Obtain a receipt from each beneficiary who receives a distribution. Be as complete as possible. If the distribution is of physical property, include a photo of the item as well as a written description on the receipt. The receipt also should be dated; state the name, address, and phone number of the beneficiary, email of the beneficiary if available, place where distribution was made, and method of distribution. Some courts have forms to be used for distribution receipts. Otherwise, you can make up your own.

Some court procedures provide for a "distribution plan" to be filed as part of the final account. If your court does this, your final accounting will include a list of the persons who will receive the assets along with a description of the assets each will receive. When the court approves the final account, the distribution plan is also approved unless objections or questions had to be resolved first. Some courts might require a separate, proposed distribution to be filed for approval after the final account, as a separate step, before actual distribution is made. Others will not need to hear from you until you have made the distribution and file your final report. As with all the forms that make up the probate steps in the administration in your court, you need to learn which steps your court requires. They are not difficult to follow, but you need to know in advance when and how you can distribute the assets. In the Estate of Little in Chapter 3, the local court in Lorain County had an option with its Fiduciary Account to distribute the assets, and that is the option Charlie Lightfoot chose. In that case, Charlie had only two other interested parties who signed a waiver of hearing on the Fiduciary's Account. Moreover, Charlie filed the Fiduciary Account after six months had passed since Jason's death; so all creditors were foreclosed from any claims under Ohio law.

When distribution of the assets is completed, you can apply to the court for an order discharging you as the personal administrator by using the forms and procedure prescribed by your court. At minimum, this will include a report of the distribution to the beneficiaries with the receipts you obtained.

When there are sufficient assets to pay off all the bills and complete the distribution according to the will, you will have few if any bumps in the road while administering the estate from opening to closure. Some issues can arise, however, especially if the testator drafted the will many years before death. Life happens in between to change the testator's property and heirs. The next several sections will cover some of the issues you might run into when attempting to finalize an estate.

Lapse of beneficiary

Under the common law, the beneficiary named in the will must survive the testator to be entitled to the bequest. If a beneficiary dies before the testator, the gift in the will "lapses." It is void. The bequest to that beneficiary becomes part of the residue of the estate. The testator, though, might have wanted or even expected the bequest to pass on to the heirs of the beneficiary. Another problem with a lapsed bequest arises if the testator failed to include a residuary clause or failed to name a contingent beneficiary for the residue and the residuary beneficiary was the one who died first. In this situation, all the property that makes up the residue of the estate becomes "intestate," something the testator probably never intended. Nevertheless, due to the death of the designated beneficiary before the testator, this is the result.

To solve this thorny problem every state except Louisiana has enacted a probate law called an "anti-lapse statute." This statute provides for certain heirs of the beneficiary to inherit the bequest instead. This usually means lineal descendants, such as children and grandchildren. For example, Wilfred bequests $10,000 to William. The rest and residue of his estate goes to William's wife,

Greta. William dies two months before Wilfred, who does not think about changing his will before he dies. In their state, the anti-lapse statute provides for the deceased beneficiary's lineal descendants to inherit in his place. William has a daughter, Wilma, who is living. Wilma becomes the beneficiary of the $10,000 bequest in Wilfred's will because the gift to her father, William, has not been permitted to lapse by law. If Wilfred's state did not have an anti-lapse statute, the $10,000 would fall under the residuary clause of his will and go to Greta.

The missing asset — ademption

Sometimes an asset named in the will cannot be found. The testator might have sold it or lost it. It might have been stolen or broken. If the asset no longer is in the estate because the testator gave it to the beneficiary named in the will intending to reduce the beneficiary's inheritance, the event is called "ademption by satisfaction." This means that the beneficiary received an "advance" on the estate. This is hard to prove, though, especially if the gift was made several years in advance of the testator's death, unless the testator left something in writing that shows that the gift was intended as an advance inheritance.

If the item is missing but was not given to the beneficiary named in the will, then it is called "ademption by extinction." The beneficiary gets nothing.

The estate representative should document by written notes all attempts to locate an item specifically listed in the will that cannot be found. The beneficiary who is named to receive it will likely not be happy if no one can recall or explain what happened to the item during the testator's lifetime and might petition the court to dispute the item's ademption and claim equivalent compensation from the estate.

Insufficient assets — abatement

1. If there are not enough assets left after payment of the estate's expenses and debts to satisfy the specific bequests in the will, the distribution is reduced by a proportionate process according to the will or otherwise state statute. This is called abatement. If the will does not direct how gifts are to be abated, most abatement statutes provide the following order of abatement. The first assets to be redirected to pay debts and expenses are any intestate assets in the estate. Although this does not often happen under a properly drafted will, there are circumstances when it might happen, such as a situation in which the testator failed to provide a backup residuary beneficiary and was predeceased by his designated residuary beneficiary.

2. If no intestate assets exist or they are insufficient, the next part of the estate to be used is the residue.

3. The next assets to be used are general legacies in the will. A general legacy is a gift of money in lump sum, such as "I give $10,000 to my niece Grace."

4. The final assets subject to being used to pay debts and expenses are specific bequests. These are such bequests as a diamond ring or a Rolex.

It is important to understand the order of abatement if there is not enough to cover all the bequests in the will so a bequest such as an antique mirror or Rolex watch is not sold out of turn when other liquid assets are available to spend. The estate representative will be liable to the beneficiaries if he or she abates assets in the wrong order. Abatement would apply also, if necessary, to adjust assets to satisfy meeting a spouse's elective share to take against the will, unless all the interested parties can agree on how to divide the property to meet the equation.

Recordkeeping

Just like any other job, especially one with fiduciary duties involved, it is important that you keep a record of the estate as you managed it. The court record will contain the will and all the court filings done, but you have more than that to evidence what you did and accomplished. The following will be important for you to demonstrate, if needed, that you discharged your duties responsibly, reasonably, and lawfully.

1. Your copy of the documents filed with the court

2. Your timekeeping record

3. Worksheets notes

4. Receipts from beneficiaries on distribution

5. Correspondence to creditors, beneficiaries, and others regarding the estate

6. Property records, for maintenance, repair, storage, upkeep, and insurance

7. Insurance

8. Banking and other financial records

9. Newspaper advertisements

10. Phone records pertaining to estate business calls

11. Photos of the inventory of estate assets

12. Appraiser(s) name, address, and phone numbers

13. Tax records

14. Background records, documents you have from decedent's files

15. Decedent's mail you received that is not in one of the above

16. Estate mail you received that is not in one of the above

If you kept computer records, copy everything onto a CD-ROM to keep with your paper file on the estate.

Closure of the Estate

Final Accounting or a similar form, when approved and discharged by the court, closes the estate. Once the estate is closed, and you are discharged as the personal representative, you no longer have any authority — or responsibility — for the estate. Sometimes a lost or hidden estate asset surfaces after an estate is closed, which requires probate for determination of its rightful disposition. In such a case, it is up to the decedent's survivors to petition the court to reopen the estate to settle the matter. The original personal representative is not required to serve again, though you could. The court will appoint a person to handle that role.

Conclusion

*N*ot unlike a part-time job during the pendency of an estate, the personal representative's work is important and can be quite fulfilling. It need not be frightening in complications. As you have seen in this book and the Appendix, more than anything else, the key is becoming familiar with a body of forms and understanding some basic governing principles that drive the probate engine.

Unless an estate is complex in property and fraught with discontent of several people, it can be handled expeditiously without a lawyer, or at least with only the occasional guidance of a lawyer for specific questions. The advantage of managing an estate hands-on is saving fees and having more involvement, which in turn can save time as well. The process also can provide a newfound insight to the workings of the legal system.

The greatest truth about serving as the personal representative of an estate is its finality. More than anything else in how modern life is conducted, handling a person's estate puts life in perspective. It also provides the estate's representative a singular opportunity, in thought and deed — which in no small part include earnest attention to the smallest detail — to commit a final act of devotion for another person.

State Facts and Figures

States with Inheritance Tax

The following currently are states that levy inheritance taxes.*

State	Spouses exempt?	Descendants exempt?	Domestic partners exempt?	Tax rate	Tax form	Deadline for filing after Date of Death
Indiana	Yes	No	No	1% to 20%	Form IH-6	9 months
Iowa	Yes	Yes	No	5% to 15%	Form IA 706	9 months
Kentucky	Yes	Yes	No	4% to 16%	Form 92A200, 92A202, or 92A205	18 months
Maryland	Yes	Yes	Certain transfers	10%	Varies	Varies
Nebraska	Yes	No	No	1% to 18%	Form 500	12 months
New Jersey	Yes	Yes	Yes	11% to 16%	Form IT-R or IT-NR	8 months
Pennsylvania	Yes	No	No	4.5% to 15%	Form REV-1500	9 months

Note that life insurance proceeds are not included as taxable inheritance in any of these states.

State Estate Tax Exemption Thresholds

The following states currently levy estate taxes above the stated exemption.

STATE	2011	2012
Connecticut	$2,000,000	$2,000,000
Delaware	$5,000,000	$5,120,000
District of Columbia	$1,000,000	$1,000,000
Hawaii	$3,600,000	$3,600.000
Illinois	$2,000,000	$3,500,000
Maine	$1,000,000	$1,000,000
Maryland	$1,000,000	$1,000,000
Massachusetts	$1,000,000	$1,000,000
Minnesota	$1,000,000	$1,000,000
New Jersey	$675,000	$675,000
North Carolina	$1,000,000	$1,000,000
Ohio	$338,333	$338,333*
Oregon	$1,000,000	$1,000,000
Rhode Island	$859,350	$892,865
Tennessee	$1,000,000	$1,000,000
Vermont	$2,750,000	$2,750,000
Washington	$2,000,000	$2,000,000

No tax beginning 1/1/2013

Caution: *These tables are informational only. State tax laws are constantly changing. Please check your state law for updated information.*

Sample Wills

Sample Simple Will

LAST WILL AND TESTAMENT

OF

JOHN B. GOODE

I, John B. Goode, resident of the Town of Essex, County of Middevale, in the State of North State, being of sound mind and memory, and with understanding of all I possess, do hereby make, publish and declare this document to be my Last Will and Testament. I hereby revoke and declare null and void all Wills and Codicils previously made by me.

ARTICLE I: DECLARATIONS

I declare that I am married as of the date of this Will and that my wife's name is Georgia B. Goode. I further declare that I have two (2) adult children, namely: Cory B. Goode, my son, of Jordanville, South State, and Marlana Z. Goode-Barre of Hindville, South State.

ARTICLE II: DEBTS, EXPENSES AND TAXES

I direct my Executrix to pay all of my legally enforceable debts, funeral expenses and estate administration expenses as soon after my death as may be practicable, except that any debt or expense secured by a mortgage, pledge, or similar encumbrance on property owned by me at my death need not be paid by my estate, because there is mortgage insurance in place to cover all such encumbrances. Said mortgage insurance policies are kept with this Will to be sure there is no confusion on this point.

I further direct that my Executrix shall pay out of residuary estate all taxes (together with interest and penalties thereon, if any) assessed upon my estate, or upon any property included as part of my gross estate, whether such property passes under the provisions of this Will or otherwise.

ARTICLE III: SPECIFIC BEQUESTS

A. I bequeath my coin collection to my son Cory B. Goode if he survives me by thirty (30) days. If Cory does not survive me by thirty (30) days, I bequeath the coin collection to Cory's son, Michael J. Goode, my grandson. If Michael J. Goode also does not survive me by thirty (30) days, this coin collection bequest shall lapse and become part of my residuary estate.

B. I give and bequeath my gun collection to my daughter Marlana Z. Goode-Barre. If Marlana does not survive me by thirty (30) days, I bequeath the gun collection my grandson, Michael J. Goode. If Michael J. Goode also does not survive me by thirty (30) days, the coin collection bequest shall lapse and become part of my residuary estate.

ARTICLE IV: GENERAL BEQUEST

I give and bequeath the sum of $10,000.00 to my sister, Clovis Morris (nee Goode) of Essex, Middevale County, North State, if she survives me by thirty (30) days. If my sister, Clovis Morris does not survive me by thirty (30) days, this bequest to her shall lapse and become a part of my residuary estate.

ARTICLE V: REAL ESTATE

I give and devise to my wife, Georgia B. Goode, absolutely and free of trust or conditions, all of my right, title, and interest in and to all real estate that is deemed and is part of my probate estate, whether I own such real estate separately, jointly with her, or others, together with all property or liability insurance policies relating to such real estate. If my wife, Georgia, does not survive me by thirty (30) days, such real estate shall become part of my residuary estate.

ARTICLE VI: RESIDUARY ESTATE

A. All the rest, residue, and remainder of the property that I may own at the time of my death, whether real, tangible, intangible, personal or mixed, of whatever kind and nature and wherever situated, including all property that I may acquire or become entitled to after the execution of this Will, or other gifts made by this Will that fail for any reason, but excluding any property over or concerning which I may have any power of appointment (all hereinafter referred to as my "residuary estate"), I bequeath to my wife, Georgia B. Goode outright and free of all conditions, except that she survive me by thirty (30) days.

B. If my wife Georgia does not survive me by thirty (30) days, then I give, devise and bequeath my residuary estate, in equal shares, to my children who survive me and the surviving descendants of any of my deceased children, *per stirpes*, outright and free of conditions.

C. If none of my children or their descendants survive me, then I bequeath my residuary estate to the Charitable Fund of North State, with its principal office in Charityville, County of Merit, North State, to be used for its general charitable purposes for the benefit of residents of North State.

ARTICLE VII: APPOINTMENT OF EXECUTRIX

A. I nominate and appoint my wife, Georgia B. Goode, as Executrix of my estate under the directions of this Will. I repose my special trust and faith in her, direct that no bond or other security be required for the faithful performance of her duties or, if bond is required by the Court, that sureties thereon be waived.

B. If my wife, Georgia B. Goode, predeceases me or fails to qualify as Executrix or, having qualified, should die, resign, or become incapacitated, then I nominate and appoint my sister, Clovis Morris, as Executrix, and give her the same powers and authority as my original Executrix was given.

C. If my sister, Clovis Morris, predeceases me or fails to qualify as Executrix or, having qualified, should die, resign, or become incapacitated, then I nominate and appoint my attorney, Chelsea Smart, as Executrix, and give her the same powers and authority as my original Executrix was given.

D. In addition to any other powers that my be conferred by law, I give my Executrix under this Will, including any successor or successors thereto, those powers set forth in the North State General Statutes, any of which may be exercised without the need for court order

ARTICLE VIII: DETERMINATION OF CHILDREN AND DESCENDANTS

As used in this Will, the words "children," "descendants," and "issue" shall include children in gestation and legally adopted individuals and the descendants of legally adopted individuals, provided such adoption took place at the time the individual adopted was a minor in the jurisdiction in which the adoption took place.

ARTICLE IX: AFTER-BORN CHILDREN

If subsequent to the execution of this Will there shall be an additional child or children born to or adopted by me, I direct that such birth or adoption shall not revoke this Will and that all references herein to my children and their issue shall include both my present children and their issue and any such after-born children and their issue.

ARTICLE X: FORFEITURE PROVISION

If any beneficiary named in this Will contests the admission of this Will into probate, contests the appointment of Executrix, or institutes or joins in any proceedings as a plaintiff to contest the validity of this Will or any provision hereof (except in good faith and with probable cause), then all bequests in this Will to such beneficiary shall lapse and my estate shall be administered and distributed in all respects as though such beneficiary had not survived me.

IN WITNESS WHEREOF, I have subscribed my name to this, my Last Will and Testament, consisting of _____ pages; and, for purposes of identification, I have initialed each preceding page in the presence of two persons, signed below as my witnesses.

_____

John B. Goode

Signed, and declared by the above-named John B. Goode, in our joint presence, that this document his Last Will and Testament, and in his presence and in the presence of each other we each have signed our names hereon as witnesses on the day and year last above written, being of lawful age and competent to do so.

_____ of _____

_____ of _____

Sample Simple Will II

Last Will and Testament of Jason Little

I, Jason Little, being of sound mind and knowing the measure of all I possess, declare this document to be my last will and testament made on July 10th in the year 2011. I revoke all prior wills and codicils.

1. I name as my Executor, Charles Lightfoot, who shall serve without bond. In the event he cannot, or declines, to serve as Executor, then I name Thrifty Bank of Elyria, Ohio, to serve as Executor.

2. I direct my Executor to make sure my funeral arrangements are handled according to the prepaid instructions and arrangements I have made with Heavenly Rest Memorial Chapel of Lorain, Ohio; to pay the taxes and all debts, if any such be due, of my estate; to disburse the specific bequests and residue of my estate as I have directed herein; and to undertake all other such business as may be necessary to settle the affairs of my estate. My Executor is to be reimbursed from the estate for any and all costs he may incur in administering the estate in addition to his lawful executor's administration fees as approved by the Court.

3. Specific Bequests I: I leave to my good friend Charles Lightfoot, the following items:
   (a) all my fishing gear; and
   (b) the sum of $10,000.

4. Specific Bequests II: I leave to my nurse, Thelma Goodbody, who has cared for me during my illness, the sum of $5,000; and

5. Specific Bequests III: I leave to the Scholarship Fund of The Perch Club of Lorain, Ohio, $1,000; and

6. The rest, residue and balance of my estate, should there be any such remaining after such bequests are satisfied and debts and obligations are paid, I leave to my good friend Charles Lightfoot. If Charles Lightfoot predeceases me, then

the residue shall pass to the Lake Erie Fish and Game Preservation Club of Lorain County, Ohio.

7. Any person who makes a claim to my estate against this will (whether such person is named herein or not) in contravention of my wishes shall be forthwith disinherited and disavowed of any and all such claim and any and all bequests made to him or her in this will. It is my express intent and direction that any person who chooses to fight against my wishes and divert any of my property otherwise than as directed herein, shall not benefit from such dispute, from my estate or from this will.

Signed of my own free knowledge without any restraint upon me on this 10th day of July 2011, this, my Last Will and Testament, at 2 Pike Place, Lorain, Ohio 44052.

Jason Little

Signed in the Presence of:

MCMcConnell, who resides at 403n TR Lane, Lorain, OH 44053

Betsy Dicken, who resides at 94 Loose Stone Rd., Kipton, OH

Sample Ethical Will

(For information purposes only)

Sometimes a testator will leave behind a document with the Last Will and Testament that is called an ethical will, letter to family and friends, or other last wishes. This ethical will document is not legally binding when it is done in this fashion because its purpose is not to express last wishes about where "the property goes." It is a passage of thoughts, wisdom, love, sometimes regrets, and even negative thoughts. This type of will is done because lawyers advise that sentiments be kept to a minimum in the legal document for disposing of the property, to keep ambiguities from creeping into the will, or drawing a person's intent or mental capacity into question. Such thoughts can become rambling and intensely personal. An attorney will advise if the testator wishes to keep personal feelings out of the public record, then the ethical will puts them in a private mode.

Why might the personal representative become involved? There might be information in the ethical will that the testator has left specifically for the personal representative as guidance. "Here's how I recommend you to handle a dispute between Ethel and James over the farm tractor," for example. The ethical will is a guideline to the deceased's thinking on various subjects, which could help resolve disputes or help communicate with grieving family who need to help make decisions.

Here is a sample ethical will (hypothetical):

To my Family:

I want you to always remember how much I love you all. My being gone in my physical person does not change that. My love is here for you.

There may be some things in my Last Will & Testament some of you will not like. I have given how I did that a lot of thought and caring, so if necessary, please remember this, "Mom wants it this way."

I have my reasons.

Joyana. I know you always loved the horses and that you wanted Everest to be yours alone to have and care for and love. I know you have a bond with him. He is a wonderful horse, and, God willing, he has a lot of good years in front of him yet. But you do not live where it would be easy to care for Everest, and your new job needs your primary focus right now. It's all about priorities. This is why I have left Everest to Sally Trainer and you together in trust with a sum of money that will care for him and his training for two years. I had this all worked out with my lawyer and Sally. This way Everest stays right where he is at Sally's. You can ride him and see him as much as you can; that's all worked out, too. Sally is responsible for his day-to-day care and training. As co-trustee you have certain powers to ensure he continues well cared for over these two years, and there are things you will be able to do with Attorney Feldman if you have any concerns about Everest's welfare or if Sally can't continue with him. At the end of the two years, if you have continued to show an interest and ability to put time to Everest, he will be yours then. If you cannot, he will be worth something if he needs to be sold, and the money will go to you from his sale. This is all spelled out in a trust I have done that goes with the will, but I wanted to explain this to you myself. I knew if we talked about it, you would become upset, and I don't want that. This gives you two years to get yourself settled, and Everest is taken care of while you are doing it.

James, please stay in college. You are going to be the world's best research biologist.

My darling Carl, thank you for dealing with all the things husbands are not supposed to have to deal with while I've been sick. We hear about people being rocks in a crisis. You have always been my rock; you never needed a crisis to be your best. Please continue to be you.

Katie, our family latecomer who is now age 5, will need all of the rest of you to help her remember things. Don't let her feel guilty when she's 16 and can't remember me very well. We have lots of photos — all those times I made you wait until I got one more video clip are going to be good Katie stories. Carl, thank you for taking those photos and videos of me I hated. I still hate them, but I want Katie to see them.

I have given some things away in the past year — and yes I was in my right mind when I did it. I have a list attached. If there's any question about what happened to …? I'm guessing you'll find it on the list. If I gave away something one of you thinks you wanted, remember I probably didn't know you wanted it, and had reasons why I needed to let it go to its new home while I was still here.

Be ethical in your lives.
Be good to each other.
Tell the truth.
Use your talents.
Read poetry.
Live every day so that you can be proud of what you did that day.
Don't dwell on regrets; they use up too much energy, and believe me when I tell you that you only get just so much energy.

Much love, now and forever,

Mom

Personal Representative Resources

Time Sheet and Expenses

Date	Description of Work Done	Total Time Spent (in tenths of an hour)	Expenses Avanced or Incurred	Comment & Follow-up

Sample Letter to Creditor

[Representative's letterhead w/phone, fax and email included]

Date
Creditor's name
Creditor's address

Re: *Estate of* _____, _____County Probate Court,
Case No. _____

Dear Sir or Madam: *[If you know a person's name, it should be "Dear Mr. or Ms. _____:"]*

As you may be aware, I am the court-appointed personal representative of the Estate of _____, who died on _____. It has come to my attention that you have, or may have, a claim of money owed you by the above-referenced estate. I need to confirm the validity of your claim, the correct amount owed, and the purpose for which you claim the amount is owed to you. Before the estate can pay a claim, certain information is required.

Please forward to me at your earliest convenience the following information:

1. Confirmation of the amount you claim owed to you by the estate; if interest, penalties or other such surcharges are included in this amount, kindly itemize the amount for services or product and the amount(s) for such other charges.

2. Copy of detailed invoice for services rendered or goods sold for which you claim this amount is owed, including any and all dates

and detailed description of services provided and/or goods sold or leased to [Name of Deceased];

3. Copies of correspondence (if any) you received from or exchanged with [Name of Deceased] prior to his death concerning your claim; and

4. Copy of a signed agreement or purchase order (if any) between you and [Name of Deceased] concerning your claim.

It is important that I receive this information no later than _____. If you have any questions please do not hesitate to call me. The best time to reach me is _____ at the above phone number. Thank you for your cooperation.

Very truly yours,
ESTATE OF _____

Estate Representative's Name
Court appointed Title (*e.g. Executor, Administrator*)

Sample Letter to Financial Institution Requesting Information

[Your letterhead and phone number]

Date
Financial Institution Name
Address

Re: Estate of [Deceased's Name], Case No., Court Name
    Request for Information

Dear [Name of Bank Manager]:

I represent the Estate of _____, referenced above. A copy of my Letter of Authority from the court is enclosed for your reference. I write for information concerning whether the deceased, _____, holds any accounts of any type or description and/or a safety deposit box with your institution. If so, please advise me at your earliest convenience, so that I may proceed to handle these matters for the Estate. Thank you for your assistance.

Very truly yours,

ESTATE OF _____

Your Name

Encl.

Note: Some institutions may request a copy of the death certificate or certified copies of your letters of authority — your court appointment paper. You can provide these in a follow-up if it proves necessary. If the deceased has no safety deposit box or funds on deposit, certified documents might not be necessary simply to obtain the initial information. Also, some institutions may refer you to their legal department. If this happens, it is just their standard procedure.

Informational Videos

The following three videos (.wmv files) are available for viewing at: **www.horrycounty.org/probatecourt/estate.asp**
"Opening an Estate"
"Inventory and Appraisement"
"Closing an Estate"

Although geared for South Carolina courts, the information is useful for anyone who wishes some general knowledge about probate in the court system.

Website Resources

"All About Probate" — NC Family Law:
www.ncfamilylaw.com/download/prob04.html

"Information Needed to Do a Simple Probate or Estate Settlement " — The Caton Law Firm: **www.kcclaw.com/CM/Events/events7.asp**

"Role of the Executor" — Family Transitions:
www.familytransitions.ca/executor_role.php

"Settling Simple Estates" — Amaral & Associates:
www.amarallaw.com/settling-simple-estates

"Settling an Estate: What Do I Need To Know?" — Montana State University Extension: **http://msuextension.org/ publications/FamilyFinancialManagement/MT201004HR.pdf**

"When A Loved One Dies" — The USAA Educational Foundation: **www.usaaedfoundation.org/Life/life_551_Settling_An_Estate**

Glossary of Terms

401(k) plan. Named after the IRS code number defining this kind of plan, this retirement savings plan allows contributions to be made automatically by your employer via deductions from your paycheck, pretax. This plan only applies to for-profit businesses.

403(b) plan. The 401(k) equivalent for not-for-profit entities and is named after the IRS code number defining this kind of retirement savings plan. It allows contributions

to be made automatically by your employer via deductions from your paycheck, pre-tax.

A

adeemed. Status given to a will if property is missing from your estate that is specifically named in the will

ademption statute. State law governing the distribution of property in an estate if items are missing or adeemed

administrator. If you die without a will, the court

appoints an individual, usually a spouse or child, who will serve in the same capacity as an executor. That person will handle all the estate paperwork, prepare a list of assets, deal with likely heirs, handle claims from creditors, make payments on outstanding debt, and handle other estate-related matters.

annuity. A retirement investment account you create by contributing a specific amount of money over a predetermined period; there will be a fixed rate of return for a number of years.

>**variable annuity.** A retirement investment account you create by contributing a specific amount of money over a predetermined amount of time; the funds are invested in the stock market, so the return depends on how well or poorly the economy does.

anti-lapse. The status of a will if a beneficiary in your will dies before you do

anti-lapse statute. State law that dictates the state will intervene if the property in a will exists, but the beneficiary is no longer alive and no contingent beneficiary is named

appointment clause. A giving clause in your will that identifies the person who will manage your estate

asset. Anything a person owns or is owed; this can be money, real estate, investments, or any other tangible property

automobile insurance. The exchange of premiums for a guaranteed payment to cover the damage or loss of a motor vehicle. Medical and liability coverage also can be included.

B

bargain sale. The sale of a piece of property to a charity at a rate that is below the fair market value. The difference between the amount paid and actual value is the amount of the gift.

beneficiary. The individual(s) or group(s) that will receive the property in a will or trust. This can be a single person (a nephew), a group of people (all grandchildren), one group (Stray Cat Rescue Inc.), several groups (all community councils in your city), or a combination of any of these.

beneficial title or **equitable title.** The right of a person or institution to take possession of or benefit from the property in a trust

bequest. A legacy or gift given by a person to another person or entity through a last will and testament after the giver dies

burial trust. Provides the funds necessary to cover the cost of your burial (or cremation) arrangements; this can be a revocable trust, but after your death, it becomes irrevocable, and the trust cannot be used for anything else.

bypass trust. A trust that transfers property to someone other than your spouse, such as a child or grandchild, but allow him or her to still benefit from the property in the trust.

C

certified public accountant (CPA). A person who has gone through professional training and meets state requirements for both education and work experience, passed a national accounting exam, and met other licensing requirements to perform the tasks of accounting such as performing audits, preparing tax returns, and giving advice to their clients — individuals or businesses — on financial matters. Accountants also can specialize in various aspects of financial estate matters, such as trusts, annuities, and estate tax law. But they also serve as estate-planning specialists that can help you consider all financial decisions.

charitable trust. A method for giving charitable institutions gifts, including regular support on a time-release basis, that are tax-free for the donor.

charitable remainder trust. Gives gifts of interest income that are paid to specific beneficiaries, such as the charity or a spouse, for a specific period; at the end of that period, the charity receives whatever is left in the trust.

charitable lead trust. Also known as a front trust; gives the charity a specific gift before all other beneficiaries receive anything

clauses. Sections in your will that organize the information in a specific order

coach. Trained professionals that specialize in offering financial, professional, and personal guidance to help you identify and manage monetary, career, and personal

goals. There are certification courses for various forms of coaching, but there are no national standards, and formal training is not required to present oneself as a coach.

codicil. A separate legal document that adds provisions to your existing will

cost-of-living adjustment. A plan variable that will allow for annual increases in the payments made to the employee to help cover the cost of rising prices. Not all plans have this feature.

Crummey trust. A complicated trust normally set up in conjunction with an irrevocable life insurance trust to make the payments for a life insurance policy; this kind of trust requires an estate-planning attorney.

custodian account. This account for minor children, which can be in the form of a trust, allows you to deposit money or property in an account set up by a bank or brokerage firm. You can name yourself as the custodian, or trustee, of the account while you are alive and then name a successor to take over those responsibilities after you die.

Uniform Gifts to Minors Act (UGMA). The first federal regulation that defined and allows an account, or trust, to be set up for minor children; some states still have this form of the law on their books.

Uniform Transfer for Minors Act (UTMA). The most current federal regulation that defines and allows an account, or trust, to be set up for minor children; if a state adopted this regulation, it served to repeal their UGMA statute.

D

decedent. A person who has died

disability insurance. An insurance policy that will make payments to you to cover living expenses and replace your lost income as a result of your inability to hold a job.

short-term disability. Provides benefits for about three months; some plans go a little longer, but only for a short period.

long-term disability. Can provide benefits for years but does eventually end, frequently at age 65 when you become eligible for Social Security

disclaimer. Refusal of a beneficiary to accept the gift given; recognized by both federal and state authorities if given in writing by a specific deadline, typically nine months after the donor's death

discretionary trust. Gives a trustee the ability to distribute income and property to a variety of beneficiaries; he or she also has the option to control the distributions to a single beneficiary as he or she decides is appropriate.

distribution. The disbursement or payment of property from an account to a beneficiary; it could be in the form of a check or some other monetary payment or the transfer of a title into the name of the beneficiary.

distribution provisions. Any clause that identifies to whom the income will be given and the frequency of those distributions, such as payments made every April 15 to the IRS

DNR. Do not resuscitate; an advance medical directive that expresses your wish to not be resuscitated or revived if you appear to have died.

donee. The person or institution receiving a gift

donor. The person who gives a gift or bequest

dumpster diving. Slang term used to describe the act of digging through trash to find bills, bank statements, or other documents with account information or any personal information that might be useful to an identity thief; this is not considered an act of theft because the U.S. Supreme Court ruled that anything left out for trash collection is in the public domain.

durable power of attorney. Allows an authorized person to act on behalf of the grantor of that power of attorney

dynasty trust. Also known as a wealth trust; can last for several generations or be set up to never end. This kind of trust helps people with a vast amount of wealth control the distribution of that money and property over a long period.

E

educational trust. A kind of protective trust that sets aside money specifically for education-related expenses, such as tuition or training fees, books, or supplies. These trusts include provisions to stop payments if the student drops out of school or flunks numerous classes.

ending clauses. These include the legalities to meet statutory requirements so that your will is legal and valid, which include (but are not limited to) your signature, date, location of the signing, and witnesses.

estate planning. Creating a set of instructions about what should be done with your things — money, possessions, investments, collectibles, or anything you own — before and after you die.

estate tax. Referred to as the "death tax" by Congress, this is the federal tax on the property in your estate after you die.

executor. Also called a personal representative, this individual handles the property you are leaving behind. If you die without a will, the court appoints an administrator, frequently a spouse or child.

exemption. A specific amount of money that will not be affected by estate taxes. Federal taxes and states with an estate tax often set an amount, such as the current $5.12 million, that is "tax-free," and then taxes are due on the amount exceeding the exempted amount.

F

family consent. Also known as a health surrogate, this is a family member designated by state law who will make medical decisions for you when you cannot do it for yourself. These laws follow a specific order of kinship for who makes a decision — if you are married, your spouse, not your sister, will be your surrogate.

family trust. A legal arrangement that involves the transfer of property from the original owner to a family member for the purpose of holding and maintaining the property until the beneficiary takes ownership

fiduciary powers clause. A giving clause in your will that includes language giving your executor the power to serve as your executor, including any duties that go beyond the basic requirements in your state regulations

financial planner. Certified Financial Planners® (CFP®), Chartered Financial Analyst (CFA), and some without initials are individuals who analyze the overall financial situation of an individual and then develop a comprehensive plan, in conjunction with the individual, that will attempt to meet his or her financial goals and objectives. Planners who are certified have followed a specific course of education or training classes, and some go on to develop expertise in specific areas such as estate or retirement planning.

funding a trust. The placement of property in a trust; that same property will be called "trust principal" once it is under the auspices of the trust agreement.

G

generation-skipping tax transfer (GSTT). A federal tax levied on property transferred to a person one or more generations removed from the donor

generation-skipping transfer trust. A tax-saving trust that is designed to benefit multiple generations after you are gone

gift tax. A federal tax levied against any property you give to another person or institution during a fiscal year; it can be in cash or the transfer of property, such as real estate or jewelry.

giving clauses. Explain what property goes to which person and under what circumstances. Real property clauses are statements that match up property with a person. Personal property clauses are used when you want to be explicit in your instructions. A residuary clause addresses the "leftovers" in your estate that you do not single out in a clause; this clause is essential for any kind of will to make sure that anything you forget or acquire since the will was prepared can be distributed. Making one or two beneficiaries is a good idea to keep your assets out of the hands of the courts.

grantor-retained trust. Irrevocable, non-charitable trusts set up in a way that is similar to a charitable trust, but the beneficiary is not a charity. There are three common types.

GRAT. A grantor-retained annuity trust gives a fixed amount of money at predetermined times, often at regularly scheduled intervals

GRIT. A grantor-retained incomes trust designates specific people to receive certain property, such as stocks or a house, but the income or use of the property stays with you until your death

GRUT. A grantor-retained unit trust pays a specific percentage to the beneficiary

gross estate. The value of all property owned by the deceased person on the date of that person's death; this portion of the estate is taxed.

guardian. The person legally appointed to be responsible for the needs of minor children until they reach a legal age; also, any adult who can be legally appointed to manage the affairs of an incompetent or infirmed adult of any age

guardianship clause. The appointment of a guardian for minor children (under the age of 18); a successor guardian also should be named as a backup.

H

health care power of attorney.
Also known as medical power of attorney, designates a person who makes medical decisions for you when you cannot do it for yourself.

heir. The legal title of a person who inherits property from an estate that does not have a will, or is intestate; beneficiaries are those who receive an inheritance by being named in a legal document such as a will or trust.

holographic will. A handwritten document signed by you but not witnessed by anyone else. Some states recognize a handwritten will as valid; others do not, so you need to check your state laws to find out if this type of will is valid in your state.

homeowner's insurance. The exchange of premiums for a guaranteed payment to cover the loss of a house and other personal property in the residence. Other coverage also can be included, such as personal liability.

homestead exemption statute. State law that protects a family home from being sold to pay off creditors if there is not enough money in an estate to cover outstanding debt

I

individual retirement account (IRA). An investment account you set up for yourself for retirement savings. Contributions you can make annually are limited. There is a tax deduction for making these contributions every year, so, technically, they are tax-free contributions.

Roth IRA. Named after its primary legislative sponsor, Senator William Roth of Delaware. Contributions to this IRA are also tax deductible in the year they are made, and taxes are paid when the money is withdrawn. The interest earned while the money is invested will be tax-free if you own the Roth IRA for at least five years.

inheritance tax. A state tax levied on the property received by a beneficiary

insurance. A method of protecting valuables in the form of a policy in which premiums are paid over time to guarantee a specific payment for a specific purpose by the company accepting the premiums. Those valuables can be property, such as your home, car, or jewelry; a person; the ability to work and care for yourself; life; health care; and long-term care.

insurance agent. An individual authorized by an insurance company to represent that company when dealing with an applicant for insurance, be it a medical, disability, dental, or long-term care policy. An agent can help you with your policy purchase by assessing the kind and amount of insurance you need and can afford.

intestate. To die without a will

inter vivos trust. A trust set up to take effect during your lifetime, before your death

irrevocable. A trust that cannot be changed, no matter what

J

joint will. One legal document for any two people, such as you and your spouse. The problem with this kind of will is that it is irrevocable, which means it cannot be changed after one of the two parties dies. The reason is that all decisions must be made by both people. A lawyer can tell you when this kind of will is a good idea, but most suggest separate wills to avoid complications.

joint-with-survivor pension. When an employee dies, his or her benefits will be paid to his or her spouse for the remainder of the spouse's life.

If the spouse waives that right, then the employee's pension payments will be larger (no need to set aside extra money for future payments), and the pension payments end when the employee dies.

K

Keogh plan. Pronounced "key-oh," this is a qualified retirement plan for sole proprietors and partners but also can be used by employees. The restrictions, distributions, and other details are similar to a defined contribution plan or defined benefit plan.

"kiddie tax." The nickname used to describe an income tax applied to money that minors did not earn through employment, also called unearned income. The special laws passed in 1996 were created to close a loophole that allowed parents to give their children a large gift as a way to pay a lower tax on the interest earned; the child tax rate was significantly lower than the adult rate.

L

lawyer. An individual who has completed a course of study in the law and passed a state certification exam that authorizes him or her to practice law and/or give legal advice. Also called attorneys, these people can specialize in specific aspects of estate planning, such as wills, trusts, or probate court, or they might have a more broad focus, such as estate planning or tax law.

legal title. Legal position that gives the trustee ownership of the property in a trust for the duration of the trustee's responsibility

liability. A debt or an obligation to pay money to another person or institution

life insurance. A financial arrangement in which an individual makes payments on a policy that guarantees the payment of a specific amount of money to a beneficiary upon the death of the person who is covered by the policy

living trust. Created while you are still alive, this trust allows you to be the grantor, trustee, and beneficiary if you choose; this is considered a "will substitute" as a way to avoid probate.

living will. Also known as a *medical directive*, you spell out the decisions you have made about your medical care while you are still alive in this legal document.

long-term care insurance. Insurance that provides payments to cover the cost of medical care. In-home nursing or nursing-home fees are examples of what might be covered.

M

marital dedication trust. Puts property into a trust that is exclusively for your spouse, who decides what happens to the property after your death

medical insurance. Frequently referred to as health insurance by those who sell it, the insurance that covers medical costs when you are sick and trying to cure an illness, injured, pregnant, and for regular checkups

Medicaid. State-run medical insurance plan that is supported by federal funding and provides medical benefits that are minimal for the financially needy. To qualify for this plan, you have to possess no more than a set dollar amount in property.

Medicare. A medical insurance program offered by the federal government to people 65 or older, certain disabled people under the age of 65, and anyone with permanent kidney failure.

Part A of this coverage is hospital insurance and **Part B** is medical insurance.

Part B now comes with a monthly premium.

medical power of attorney. Also known as health care power of attorney; designates of person who makes medical decisions for you when you cannot do it for yourself.

minor trust. A way to give gifts to a minor that avoids the gift tax and keeps the property safe until the minor becomes an adult and can take ownership of the trust

marital trust. A trust for the surviving legal spouse of the deceased

mutual will. A plan for your estate prepared in conjunction with another person

N

net worth. A person's true financial value. Assets – Liabilities = Net Worth.

non-charitable trust. A trust that has a person or institution that is not a charity as the beneficiary

non-statutory living will. A legal document in which you spell out the decisions you have made about your medical care while you are still alive that does not comply with the laws of your state. A statutory document likely will provide more protection for the physicians and nurses carrying out your wishes.

nuncupative will. Also called an oral will, this is a spoken will. Some states only allow this kind of will if someone is literally on their deathbed, and it only covers personal property of little or no value. Again, you need to check with your state on the laws regarding this kind of will.

O

opening clauses. Lay out the basic information about whom the will is for and set the stage for the clauses that follow. The *introductory clause* identifies the person making the will, the *family statement clause* introduces and identifies the family members that will be referred to later in the will, and the *tax clause* explains how the taxes on the estate will be paid.

outright charitable gift. Property given to a charity; the gift can be cash or any other type of property.

ownership. The individual(s) who hold the legal title to a piece of property; the ability to retain, sell, or give away this property depends on the number of people who hold that title, in some cases, their relationship, and any legal agreements/contracts connected to the property.

    community property. A state law that views a wife and husband as equal partners and assumes a 50/50 split of ownership

    joint ownership. When any two people hold an equal share of the title to a piece of property; the most common form is spousal, or when a legally married couple has both names on a title to a piece of property.

    joint tenancy. A group of people hold an equal and undivided title to a piece of property

    separate property. Things owned by one spouse that are not part of the couple's community property

    sole ownership. A single person holds the title to the property.

P

payable on death (POD). An account, like a savings account, that has a specific stipulation that the death of the original owner automatically transfers the ownership to a named beneficiary.

Pension Benefit Guaranty Corporation (PBGC). A federal agency that can insure and therefore protect some or all your pension, if your plan qualifies for the coverage and your company purchases the insurance

pension plan. A program set up by an employer, including government agencies, to pay employees benefits upon retirement. Each employee has an individual account, and the employer contributes to each employee's account based on the terms of the plan. There are two common types of pension plans.

defined benefit plan. A plan in which the employee will receive a specified amount of money upon retirement; the amount of the disbursement made is based on the number of years of employment.

defined contribution plan. A pension plan that sets a specific amount an employee will put into the plan (a percentage of income) and makes payments only for the amount of money contributed to the plan.

pour-over will. This will place some property into a trust that was established while the decedent was still alive.

probate court. The state level court system that is specifically set up to handle all matters related to the distribution of a deceased person's estate; this is where a will is filed and unanswered questions about the disbursement of an estate are settled by a judge.

profit sharing plan. Employees receive a portion of the profits earned by the company; the plan determines the amount that will be contributed to each employee's account.

property. Also referred to as personal property, this comprises your possessions. This category is further divided into.

intangible personal property. Checking accounts, savings accounts, money market funds, mutual funds, stocks, bonds, or retirement accounts such as a pension, an IRA, a Roth IRA, or a Keogh plan

real property. Any kind of real estate, such as a house, a condo, or a vacant lot

tangible personal property. Things you can touch, such as a signed baseball, jewelry, or linen bed sheets.

property guardian. Also known as a property manager, a legal adult who takes responsibility for the oversight of property inherited by a minor/child. Children under the age of 18 can inherit property, but they can only be allowed to legally own that property with adult supervision; an adult must have the responsibility of managing it.

property interest. This refers to the connection a person has to a specific item, piece of land, or other items.

beneficial interest. You receive a benefit from the property.

legal interest. Property a person can legally transfer or manage, but the individual does not own it. Someone who is responsible for the maintenance and oversight of the use of a piece of property but who does not legally own it is called a trustee.

protective trust. a trust designed with conditions to protect the beneficiary's property.

provisions. Clauses that explain how you want your wishes carried out

Q

QTIP. A qualified terminable interest property trust is a marital deduction trust, but instead of your spouse deciding who gets the property after your death, the grantor makes that decision.

qualified pension plan. A plan in which the amount of money that the employer puts into an employee's account is not taxed as income during the fiscal year the contribution is made.

R

renter's insurance. The exchange of premiums for a guaranteed payment to cover the loss of personal property housed in rental property that is used as a primary residence.

revocable trust. A trust that can be changed.

S

simple will. A legal document that identifies who you are, your beneficiaries, your executor, the directions you leave for the care of people for whom you are responsible, and the distribution of your assets.

Social Security Disability Benefit. Monthly payment made by the federal government to qualified recipients who can no longer work. Payments are made until the age of 65; at that point, you begin to receive the social security retirement benefit at the same rate.

Social Security Retirement Benefit. Monthly payment made by the federal government to qualified recipients who reach retirement age. Payments are based on contributions made during the individual's employment period.

Social Security Supplemental Security Income (SSI). The federal government makes a monthly payment to qualified individuals. This benefit is for people who have little (if any) property or are blind or disabled in some other way.

special needs trust. A support trust for a disabled person under the age of 65 (you or anyone else). This trust makes payments on the beneficiaries' behalf, as required by the state as reimbursement.

After the beneficiary dies, the property in the trust is paid to other beneficiaries. This trust is designed to protect your property from seizure by the government or a creditor seeking reimbursement.

special provisions. Encompasses all clauses that create specific requirements unique to the beneficiary or the assets. For example, a beneficiary of a trust might be required to be 21 or graduate college before he or she can take ownership of that trust.

spendthrift trust. A trust set up for someone who will not be able to handle his or her own affairs or who is mentally incompetent or might have financial problems and needs protection from creditors. The beneficiary does not own the property in the trust, just the payments that are made from the trust.

spiritual adviser. A minister, priest, monk, or some other cleric or individual trained in a specific faith tradition that offers guidance, support, and information related to their belief system.

split-interest trust. More than one individual benefits from the trust. One person or charity would have an interest in the trust for a specific time, and then another person or charity receives the property that remains.

state estate tax. A tax levied by the state on property left in an estate after a person dies, similar to the estate tax by the federal government, but the state tax is an additional tax burden. Not all states have an estate tax.

state gift tax. A tax by individual states according to terms they set that is levied against any property you give to another person or institution during a fiscal year; it can be in cash or the transfer of property such as real estate or jewelry. Many of these are tied in some way to the federal estate tax.

state income tax. A tax on income earned during a fiscal year that is for residents of that state. Income earned in another state might be taxable in your state of residence, and any inheritance you receive that counts as income and is entered on your federal tax form can also be taxed.

statutory living will. A legal document in which you spell out the decisions you have made about your medical care while you are still alive that complies with the statutes or laws of your state. A statutory document likely will provide more protection than a non-statutory living will for the physicians and nurses carrying out your wishes.

stock bailout. The transfer of stock ownership from your name to that of a charity; the fair market value of the stock at the time of the transfer is the gift amount.

stock bonus plan. A retirement plan established by an employer to give shares of the company's stock to employees. When the employee receives the shares, he must pay taxes based on the value of the stock.

employee stock ownership plan (ESOP). A retirement type of stock bonus plan. The employer contributes shares of its stock to a qualified trust, and the employee only pays taxes based on distributions she receives.

successor trustee. Someone who will step in if the primary trustee is unable to serve or cannot continue to manage your trust. This person will have the same legal obligations for managing the trust as the original trustee, should the successor assume the management responsibilities.

supplemental needs trust. A support trust for a handicapped, elderly, or disabled person in need of support is assisted by this trust in such a way that it does not reduce or jeopardize the eligibility of that person to receive public or private benefits. This trust is designed to protect your property from seizure by the government or a creditor seeking reimbursement.

support trust. Requires a trustee to pay only the income and property necessary to cover the cost of education or assistance such as health care or nursing home fees of the beneficiaries

survival clause. Leaves everything in your estate to one named person. Married people frequently do this to ensure that everything goes to the surviving spouse.

survivor benefit. A portion of the deceased employee's pension paid to the surviving spouse. The amount, regularly a percentage, is set by the terms of the pension plan rules.

T

tax-deferred. Taxes on money put into an investment account are paid when it is received by the employee in the form of a distribution, not at the time the money goes into the account.

term insurance. A life insurance policy that carries an annual premium and pays a specified death benefit to the beneficiary but does not have a cash value, so you cannot borrow money from it. The only payment made is to the beneficiary. The death benefit is not paid if premium payments are stopped.

annual renewable. A term life policy that has an annual premium and can be renewed from year to year

decreasing. A term life policy in which premiums remain the same but the benefit decreases over time. For example, if you purchase this kind of insurance (also called mortgage or credit term insurance) to pay off your debts after you die, the mortgage you want to insure might be $250,000 at the time you purchase the insurance, but the mortgage value when you die might be $150,000. The policy then pays $150,000. This kind of insurance is recommended only for those who cannot get any other kind of insurance.

group. Employers frequently purchase a term life policy for each employee as an added benefit. Employees get an excellent low rate, and there is no income tax on the premiums for the first $50,000 of coverage.

level. A term life policy with coverage that is guaranteed for a specific period, or term, such as five, ten, or 20 years at a specific premium. The premium will remain for the five-year period, but at year six, it will go up and remain at that rate through the tenth year, continuing after that.

testamentary trust. A fund created by the terms of your will after your death

testamentary trust will. This will moves your assets into one or more trusts after your death.

testator. A person who writes a will

Totten trust. A bank account that, upon your death, immediately passes to the named beneficiary

trust. A legal arrangement that involves the transfer of property from the original owner to a person or a company for the purpose of holding and maintaining the property for the benefit of a specific individual, group of people, or institution(s)

trustee. The person or company that will oversee or manage a financial resources account, such as a trust or custodian account, once it is established or that manages a trust in which the trustor has placed money or property to be held for the benefit of persons named as beneficiaries of the trust. This person or group will make sure the property in the trust is safe and in good order until it is turned over to the beneficiaries.

trust agreement. The legal document that spells out the terms of a trust, including the people and conditions and the rules that must be followed; some are state or federal laws, and others are specific conditions.

trustor. The person who sets up the trust. Other names commonly used are creator, donor, settlor, or grantor.

trust principal. The name given to property that is placed into a trust and is managed by trustees under the terms of a trust agreement.

U

umbrella liability insurance. The exchange of premiums for a guaranteed payment to cover a host of situations that would put personal property at risk, such as personal liability or negligence

V

vested. To meet the predetermined requirements contained within a pension plan based on the number of years you have worked for the employer. Before an employee can receive any distributions or take full ownership of a pension plan, the employee has to be fully vested.

W

waiver. A written statement declining the right to receive benefits signed by a spouse. This waiver must be signed to legally sever the right to claim any benefits — an alternative agreement, such as signing a prenuptial agreement, will not be enough.

whole life insurance. Sometimes called "cash value"

life insurance, this is a form of life insurance for which the insured person pays a monthly or annual premium to a company that will, upon the owner's death, pay a predetermined, fixed amount of money to the beneficiaries. A portion of the fixed (meaning it will never go up or down) premium is invested, another portion is placed into an account, like a savings account, and that cash value is accessible to the policy owner. It can be borrowed against as a loan, or the cash can be taken as the proceeds of the policy instead of the death benefit payout.

joint first-to-die or second-to-die. Just as it sounds, this is a policy held by two people, and the beneficiary is paid after the first or second person dies, as designated in the policy.

universal life. A kind of whole life policy that guarantees a minimum return, but the value of the policy can go up or down. If the policy makes more money, the return might be high enough to cover your premium payments.

will. A legal document in which you identify what people or institutions will receive money and property from your estate after your death; it also serves to appoint guardianship of children or adults who are your legal responsibility and designates an executor to manage your estate after you die.

will substitute. An agreement, contract, or other legal arrangement that will accomplish the same goals of a will — to protect and transfer property rights — but without the use of a will document.

Bibliography

Alaska Probate Code. Accessed July 31, 2011. **www. estatefinance.com/alaska_probate_code.php**.

Alabama Probate Code. Accessed July 30, 2011. **http://law.justia. com/codes/alabama/2006/30792/130738.html**.

Arizona Probate Code. Accessed July 31, 2011. **www.azleg.gov/ ArizonaRevisedStatutes.asp?Title=14**.

Arkansas Probate Code. Accessed July 31, 2011. **www. lexisnexis.com/hottopics/arcode/Default.asp**.

Calhoun County Probate Court, *Jacksonville News*, "Notice to Creditors State of Alabama Calhoun County Probate Court Case No. 29611 In the Matter of the Estate of Reinalodo Antonio Boyd, Deceased." Accessed July 31, 2011. **www.jaxnews.com/ pages/ad_details/listing_details?id=19596388-notice-to-**

creditors-state-of-alabama-calhoun-county-probate-court-case-no-29611-in-the-matter-of-the-estate-of-reinalodo-antonio-boyd-deceased.

California Probate Code. Accessed July 30, 2011. **www.leginfo.ca.gov/cgi-bin/calawquery?codesection=prob**.

Chippewa County, Wisconsin, Probate Website. Accessed May 26, 2011. **www.co.chippewa.wi.us/index.php?option=com_content&view=article&id=350&Itemid=444**.

Colorado Probate Code. Accessed July 31, 2011. **www.michie.com/colorado/lpext.dll?f=templates&fn=main-h.htm&cp**.

Connecticut Probate Code. Accessed July 31, 2011. **www.cga.ct.gov/2011/pub/title45a.htm**.

Delaware Probate Code. Accessed July 31, 2011. **http://delcode.delaware.gov/title12/index.shtml**.

District of Columbia Probate Code. Accessed July 31, 2011. **http://government.westlaw.com/linkedslice/default.asp?SP=DCC-1000**.

Florida Probate Code. Accessed July 31, 2011. **www.flsenate.gov/Laws/Statutes/?from500=yes**.

Garber, Julie. "Overview of Current Federal Estate Tax Laws." About.com. 2011. Accessed July 25, 2011. **http://wills.about.com/od/understandingestatetaxes/a/overviewfed.htm**.

Georgia Probate Code. Accessed July 31, 2011. **www.lexisnexis.com/hottopics/gacode/Default.asp**.

Greenville County, N.C., Probate Court Website, Online Forms. Accessed July 25, 2011. **www.greenvillecounty.org/probate/ estate_forms.asp**.

Hawaii Probate Code. Accessed July 31, 2011. **www.capitol.hawaii.gov/hrscurrent/vol12_ch0501-0588/ hrs0560/hrs_0560-.htm**.

Idaho Probate Code. Accessed July 31, 2011. **www.legislature.idaho.gov/idstat/Title15/T15.htm**.

Illinois Probate Code. Accessed July 31, 2011. **www.ilga.gov/legislation/ilcs/ilcs2.asp?ChapterID=60**.

Indiana Probate Code. Accessed July 31, 2011. **www.in.gov/legislative/ic/code/title29/ar1**.

Iowa Probate Code. Accessed July 31, 2011. **http://search.legis. state.ia.us/NXT/gateway.dll?f=templates&fn=default.htm**.

Kansas Probate Code. Accessed July 31, 2011. **http://kansasstatutes.lesterama.org/Chapter_59**.

Kentucky Probate Code. Accessed July 31, 2011. **www.lrc.state.ky.us/KRS/396-00/CHAPTER.HTM**.

Louisiana Code of Civil Procedure. Accessed July 31, 2011. **www.legis.state.la.us/lss/lss.asp?folder=68**.

Maine Probate Code. Accessed July 31, 2011. **www.maine legislature.org/legis/statutes/18-a/title18-Ach0sec0.html**.

Maryland Statutes. Accessed July 31, 2011.
http://mlis.state.md.us/asp/web_statutes.asp.

Massachusetts Probate Code. Accessed July 31, 2011.
www.malegislature.gov/Laws/GeneralLaws/PartII/TitleII/
Chapter190B.

Michigan Court Forms, courts.michigan.gov. "Notice To
Creditors Decedent's Estate." Accessed July 20, 2011.
http://courts.michigan.gov/Administration/SCAO/Forms/
Pages/default.aspx.

Michigan Laws. Accessed July 31, 2011.
www.legislature.mi.gov.

Minnesota Probate Laws. Accessed July 31, 2011.
www.revisor.mn.gov/statutes/?view=part&start=524&clo
se=532.

Mississippi Probate Code. Accessed July 31, 2011.
www.mscode.com/free/statutes/91/index.htm.

Missouri Probate Code. Accessed July 31, 2011.
www.moga.mo.gov/STATUTES/STATUTES.HTM#T31.

Montana Probate Code. Accessed July 31, 2011.
http://data.opi.mt.gov/bills/mca_toc/72.htm.

Nebraska Probate Statutes. Accessed July 31, 2011. http://
uniweb.legislature.ne.gov/laws/browse-chapters.
php?chapter=30.

Nevada Revised Statutes. Accessed July 31, 2011.
www.leg.state.nv.us/NRS/Index.cfm.

New Hampshire Probate Statutes. Accessed July 31, 2011.
www.gencourt.state.nh.us/rsa/html/NHTOC/NHTOC-LVI.htm.

New Jersey Permanent Statutes. Accessed July 31, 2011.
http://lis.njleg.state.nj.us/cgi-bin/om_isapi.dll?clientID=355134&depth=2&expandheadings=off&headingswithhits=on&infobase=statutes.nfo&softpage=TOC_Frame_Pg42.

New Mexico Probate Code. Accessed July 31, 2011. **http://law.justia.com/codes/new-mexico/2006/nmrc/jd_ch45-e75.html**.

New York State Laws. Accessed July 31, 2011.
http://assembly.state.ny.us/leg/?cl=38.

North Carolina General Statutes. Accessed May 21, 2012.
http://www.ncleg.net/gascripts/statutes/statutestoc.pl.

North Dakota Probate Code. Accessed May 21, 2012.
http://www.legis.nd.gov/cencode/t30-1.html.

Ohio Probate Code. Accessed May 15, 2012.
http://codes.ohio.gov/orc/21.

Oregon Probate Code. Accessed May 17, 2012.
www.leg.state.or.us/ors/111.html.

Pennsylvania Probate Code. Accessed May 21, 2012.
www.legis.state.pa.us/WU01/LI/LI/CT/PDF/20/20.PDF.

Rhode Island Probate Code. Accessed May 21, 2012.
www.rilin.state.ri.us/Statutes/TITLE33/INDEX.HTM.

South Carolina Probate Code. Accessed May 21, 2012.
www.scstatehouse.gov/code/title62.php.

South Dakota Probate Code. Accessed May 21, 2012.
http://legis.state.sd.us/statutes/DisplayStatute.
aspx?Type=Statute&Statute=29A.

Texas Probate Code. Accessed January 18, 2012.
www.texasprobatelawfirm.com/code.html.

Walters, Melanie. "Florida Probate: Does Probate Law
require you to hire a Florida Probate Attorney?" February
17, 2009. Accessed May 10, 2011. www.obituarieshelp.org/
articles/florida_probate_does_probate_law_require_you_to_
hire_a_florida_probate_attorney.html.

Washington Probate Code. Accessed May 21, 2012.
http://apps.leg.wa.gov/rcw/default.aspx?Cite=11.

West Virginia Probate Code. Accessed May 21, 2012.
http://law.justia.com/codes/west-virginia/2005/41/41.html.

Winstead Law Group, APC, Laguna, CA. Website, Accessed
May 26, 2011. www.winsteadlaw.net/contact.html. (Probate
costs in California).

Author Biography

graduate of the University of Akron School of Law, Linda C. Ashar has practiced law in Ohio state and federal courts for 27 years and enjoys teaching as a part-time university professor of law and ethics courses. In addition to these pursuits, she is an artist and writer. She lives at Thornapple Farms in Vermilion, Ohio, with her lawyer-husband, Mike, where they raise rare breed horses and ponies. Ashar is senior counsel for the law firm of Wickens, Herzer, Panza Cook & Batista Co. of Avon, Ohio.

Index